Marco Cantù

Essential
Pascal

Piacenza, Italy

4th Edition, April 2008

Author and publisher: Marco Cantù.

Editor: Peter W. A. Wood

Tech Editors (for this edition): Patricio Moschcovich, Keld R. Hansen

Cover Designer: Fabrizio Schiavi

ISBN: 1440480117 (EAN-13: 9781440480119).

Delphi is a trademark of CodeGear, a subsidiary of Borland. Windows and Windows Vista are trademarks of Microsoft. Other trademarks are of the respective owners, as referenced in the text.

Edition for createspace.com. Revision 2. April 21ˢᵗ 2008.

Printed copies of this book can be ordered at http://www.marcocantu.com/epascal.

Marco Cantù, Essential Pascal

Introduction

This book is dedicated to my family,
Lella, Benedetta, and Jacopo.

The first few editions of Mastering Delphi, the best selling series of Delphi books that I wrote between 1995 and 2005, provided an introduction to the Pascal language in Delphi. Due to space constraints and because many Delphi programmers looked for more advanced information, this material was completely omitted in the later editions of the Mastering Delphi series. To overcome the absence of this information, I started putting together an ebook, titled "Essential Pascal". After several online "only" editions I'm now making the book available in three formats, a free HTML-based book (with ads), a paid PDF-based version, and a printed book. I've kept the prices of the PDF and print version very low, to suit an audience of students and hobbyists, although the book can serve professional developers as well.

Pascal, as in Delphi

This is a detailed book on the Pascal language found in Delphi, and in some of the available Delphi dialects (namely FreePascal and Chrome)[1]. The book

---

1   There is also a GNU Pascal compiler which supports the ISO 7185 and ISO 10206 standards, but it is really not commonly used by the Pascal community, which is generally tied to non-standard Borland extensions of the language.

Marco Cantù, Essential Pascal

purposely focuses on the *traditional* Pascal language constructs, not delving into its object-oriented extensions. From time to time there will be updates to cover extensions to the core language provided by recent editions of Delphi (again, not the OOP extensions of Object Pascal).

The first complete version of this book, dated July '99, was published on the Delphi 5 Companion CD. Following editions were updated, both in the content and in the format, with notes covering Kylix (Delphi for Linux) and Delphi for .NET. This new edition, the first available in print, extends coverage to other Pascal/Delphi dialects.

During the various editions, the examples used in the book were all migrated away from using Delphi's Visual Control Language (VCL) graphic user interface (GUI), to make the book better suited for different platforms and compilers. Changing the examples from visual ones to console based ones, brings with it the advantage that the reader can focus even more on the language, ignoring event handlers, methods, component, and other more advance topics. Also, the programs can run on non-Windows platforms.

Book Copyright and Availability

```
http://www.marcocantu.com/epascal
```

In the very beginning the book was HTML only. Following editions were available as PDF, which was a free download although I did ask for a volunteer-based license fee (or donation). Now I'm publishing the book in three formats (with exactly the same content):

- Free HTML version with advertising.
- PDF version you can buy on Lulu.com (if you've obtained it elsewhere this is probably an illegal copy).

- Printed version you can buy on Lulu.com.

Source Code

The source code of all the examples mentioned in the book is freely available. The code has the same copyright as the book: Feel free to use it at will but don't publish it on other documents or site. Download details and a list of examples are available in the Appendix to the book.

Feedback

Please let me know of any errors you find, but also of topics not clear enough for a beginner. Also let me know which other topics you'd like to see me cover in future books.

The preferred way of sending feedback is on my public newsgroup (see my web site *delphi.newswhat.com* for a web interface to my groups) in the area devoted to books. If you have trouble using the newsgroups email me at *marco.cantu@gmail.com*.

Acknowledgments

That I'm publishing a book on the web for free is mainly due to Bruce Eckel's experience with *Thinking in Java*. I'm a friend of Bruce and think he really did a great job with that book and few others, not only because of the high quality content of those books, but also for his experiments with the books' delivery model.

When I mentioned the project to people at Borland (as it was called at the time) I got a lot of positive feedback as well. And of course, I must thank the company for making first the Turbo Pascal series of compilers and now the Delphi series of visual IDEs.

Marco Cantù, Essential Pascal

I've received some precious feedback on early versions of the ebook. The first readers who helped improve this material were Charles Wood and Wyatt Wong. Mark Greenhaw and Frederic Gauthier-Boutin helped with some editing of the text. Rafael Barranco-Droege offered a lot of technical corrections and language editing. Thanks.

While working on this new edition I had editorial help from Peter W. A. Wood and technical reviews by Patricio Moschcovich and Keld R. Hansen. The book cover was designed by Fabrizio Schiavi. It represents a Pascal triangle[2], and matches the cover of my Delphi 2007 Handbook.

About the Author

I live in Piacenza, Italy. After teaching the C++ language and writing C++ and Object Windows Library books and articles, in 1995 I delved into Delphi programming. I'm the author of the *Mastering Delphi* book series, published by Sybex, the advanced *Delphi Developers Handbook* (which is hard to find these days, but might soon get republished by myself), and the recently published *Delphi 2007* Handbook. I have written articles for many magazines, including *The Delphi Magazine*, have spoken at Delphi and Borland conferences around the world, and given Delphi classes at basic and advanced levels.

Lately I've been getting more and more involved in Web 2.0 development techniques and XML-related technologies, although mostly from the Delphi perspective. You can find more details about me and my work on my web site,

```
http://www.marcocantu.com
```

and on my blog,

```
http://blog.marcocantu.com
```

---

2   More information on http://en.wikipedia.org/wiki/Pascal's_triangle.

Table Contents

Marco Cantù, Essential Pascal

Chapter 1: Short History Of The Pascal Language

The Object Pascal programming language we use in Delphi wasn't invented in 1995 along with the Borland visual development environment. It was simply extended from the Object Pascal language already in use in the Borland Pascal products. But Borland didn't invent Pascal, it only helped make it very popular and extended it a little.

Marco Cantù, Essential Pascal

Wirth's Pascal

The Pascal language was originally designed in 1971 by Niklaus Wirth[3], professor at the Polytechnic of Zurich, Switzerland. Pascal was designed as a simplified version, for educational purposes, of the Algol language, which dates from 1960.

When Pascal was designed, many programming languages existed, but few were in widespread use: FORTRAN, Assembler, COBOL. The key idea of the new language was order, managed through a strong concept of data types, declaration of variables and structured program controls. The language was also designed to be a teaching tool.

Turbo Pascal

Borland's world-famous Pascal compiler, called Turbo Pascal, was introduced in 1983, implementing "Pascal User Manual and Report" by Jensen and Wirth. The Turbo Pascal compiler has been one of the best-selling series of compilers of all time, and made the language particularly popular on the PC platform, thanks to its balance of simplicity and power.

Turbo Pascal introduced an Integrated Development Environment (IDE) where you could edit the code (in a WordStar compatible editor), run the compiler, see the errors, and jump back to the lines containing those errors. It sounds trivial now, but previously you had to quit the editor, return to DOS; run the command-line compiler, write down the error lines, open the editor and jump to the error lines.

Moreover Borland sold Turbo Pascal for 49 dollars, where Microsoft's Pascal compiler was sold for a few hundred. Turbo Pascal's many years of success contributed to Microsoft eventual dropping its Pascal compiler product.

You can actually download a copy of the original version of Borland's Turbo Pascal from the *Museum* section of the CodeGear's Developer Network:

```
http://dn.codegear.com/museum
```

---

3   See the official Wirth biography at http://www.cs.inf.ethz.ch/~wirth/

Delphi's Pascal

After 9 versions of Turbo and Borland Pascal compilers, which gradually extended the language into the Object Oriented Programming (OOP) realm, Borland released Delphi in 1995, turning Pascal into a visual programming language. Delphi extends the Pascal language in a number of ways, including many object-oriented extensions which are different from other flavors of Object Pascal, including those in the *Borland Pascal with Objects* compiler (the last incarnations of Turbo Pascal).

With Delphi 2, Borland brought the Pascal compiler to the 32-bit world, actually re-engineering it to provide a code generator common with the C++ compiler. This brought many optimizations previously found only in C/C++ compilers to the Pascal language.

In Delphi 3 Borland added to the language the concept of interfaces, making a leap forward in the expressiveness of classes and their relationships. With Kylix, Borland made a further step and opened to Pascal/Delphi programmers the Linux operating system (even if only in its Intel-based incarnation). Most of the examples of this book can be executed almost unchanged on Linux.

With the release of version 7 of Delphi (and version 3 of Kylix) Borland has formally started to call the Pascal (or Object Pascal) language the Delphi language. So Delphi 7 uses the Delphi language, Kylix 3 supports both the Delphi and the C++ languages, and Borland ships a Delphi language compiler for the Microsoft's .NET architecture. This is mainly a cosmetic and marketing change, probably due to the fact that the Pascal language was never popular in the US as it used to be (and still is) in Europe and other areas of the world.

Delphi 8 for .NET has introduced a new breed of Delphi IDE and added extensive support in the language and libraries for Microsoft's .NET architecture. Delphi 8, released at the end of 2003, marked the most extensive and dramatic set of changes to the Object Pascal-Delphi language since the introduction of Delphi 1 in 1995, changes that were also adopted in the Win32 Delphi compiler.

At the time of this writing, the latest version of Delphi is RAD Studio 2007, which is now produced by CodeGear, a Borland subsidiary. Among other changes, CodeGear brought back the original name of the language, which is now once again officially called Object Pascal. Most notably, CodeGear pro-

Marco Cantù, Essential Pascal

duced a solid Delphi 2007, after a "not-so-great" Delphi 2005 and a some-what unstable Delphi 2006.

Among other Delphi dialects, the two most commonly used are FPC (Free Pascal Compiler) and Chrome (a .NET-based language by RemObjects). I'll often mention these two dialects in the book. The respective web sites are:

```
http://www.freepascal.org
http://www.remobjects.com/chrome
```

Chapter 2: Coding In Pascal

This chapter describes the element of a Pascal program, like keywords, white spaces, and expressions. Here you'll find the basic building blocks of Pascal.

As a starting point, I'm going to show you the code of a simple *Hello, World* application showing some of the structural elements of a Pascal program. I won't explain what these elements mean just yet, as that is the purpose of the first few chapters of the book. Here is the code:

```pascal
program EssHello;
{$APPTYPE CONSOLE}

var
  strMessage: string;
begin
  strMessage := 'Hello, Small World';
  writeln (strMessage);
  // wait until Enter is pressed
  readln;
end.
```

Marco Cantù, Essential Pascal

You can see the program name in the first line, a compiler directive, a variable declaration, and three lines of code (plus a comment) within the main `begin-end` block. Again, we'll learn about all of these elements soon, this serves only to give you an idea of what a small but complete Pascal program looks like.

Syntax and Style

Before we move on to the subject of writing Pascal language statements, it is important to highlight a couple of elements of Pascal coding style. The question I'm addressing here is this: Besides the syntax rules, how should you write code? There isn't a single answer to this question, since personal taste can dictate different styles. However, there are some principles you need to know regarding comments, uppercase, spaces, and the so-called pretty-printing (pretty for us human beings, not the computer).

In general, the goal of any coding style is clarity. The style and formatting decisions you make are a form of shorthand, indicating the purpose of a given piece of code. An essential tool for clarity is consistency-whatever style you choose, be sure to follow it throughout a project and across projects.

Comments

In traditional Pascal, comments were enclosed in either braces or parentheses followed by a star. Modern versions also accept the C++ style comments, double slash, which can span to the end of the line and has no symbol to signal the end the comment:

```
{this is a comment}
(* this is another comment *)
// this is a comment up to the end of the line
```

The first form is shorter and more commonly used. The second form was often preferred in Europe because many European keyboards lacked the brace symbol. The third form of comment has been borrowed from C++ and was added in Delphi 2. Comments up to the end of the line are very helpful for short comments and for commenting out a single line of code[4].

Notice that in the code listings in the book, I'll try to typeset comments in italics and keywords in bold, to be consistent with the default Delphi syntax highlighting (and that of most other editors).

Having three different forms of comments can be helpful for marking nested comments. If you want to comment out several lines of source code to disable them, and these lines contain some real comments, you cannot use the same comment identifier:

```
{  ... code
{comment, creating problems}
... code }
```

With a second comment identifier, you can write the following code, which is correct:

```
{  ... code
// this comment is OK
... code }
```

Note that if the open brace or parenthesis-star is followed by the dollar sign($), it becomes a compiler directive, as in[5]:

```
{$X+}
```

Valid compiler directives are listed in the compiler documentation or help. They generally affect the way the compiler generates code and are compiler specific, certainly not part of the language as such, and too advanced to be covered here.

Use of Uppercase

Unlike other languages, including all those derived from C like C++, Java, and C#, the Pascal compiler ignores case, the capitalization of characters.

---

4   Since Delphi 2006 and Turbo Delphi you can comment or uncomment a line (or a group of lines) with a direct keystroke. This is Ctrl+/ on the US keyboard and a different combination (with the physical / key) on other keyboards.

5   Actually, compiler directives are still comments. For example, {$X+ This is a comment} is legal. It's both a valid directive and a comment, although any *sane* programmers will probably tend to separate directives and comments.

Therefore, the identifiers Myname, MyName, myname, myName, and MYNAME are all exactly the same. In my opinion, case-insensitivity is definitely a positive feature, as syntax errors and other subtle mistakes can be caused by incorrect capitalization in case-sensitive languages[6].

There are a couple of subtle drawbacks, however. First, you must be aware that these identifiers really are the same, so you must avoid using them as different elements. Second, you should try to be consistent in the use of uppercase letters, to improve the readability of the code.

A consistent use of case isn't enforced by the compiler, but it is a good habit to get into. A common approach is to capitalize only the first letter of each identifier. When an identifier is made up of several consecutive words (you cannot insert a space in an identifier), every first letter of a word should be capitalized:

```
MyLongIdentifier
MyVeryLongAndAlmostStupidIdentifier
```

This is often called "Pascal-casing", to contrast it with the so-called "Camel-casing" of Java and C-derived languages, which capitalizes internal words but requires an initial lowercase letter, like in

```
myLongIdentifier
```

White Space

Other elements completely ignored by the compiler are the spaces, new lines, and tabs you add to the source code. All these elements are collectively known as *white space*. White space is used only to improve code readability; it does not affect the compilation in any way.

Unlike traditional BASIC, Pascal allows you to write a statement on several lines of code, splitting a long instruction on two or more lines. The drawback (at least for many BASIC programmers) of allowing statements on more than one line is that you have to remember to add a semicolon to indicate the end

---

6   In Delphi there is only one exception to the case-insensitive rule of Pascal: the
    Register procedure of a components' package must start with the uppercase *R*,
    because of a C++Builder compatibility issue. Of course, when you refer to identifiers
    exported by other languages (like a native Win32 function or a .NET class) you might
    have to use the proper capitalization.

of a statement, or more precisely, to separate a statement from the next one. The only restriction in splitting programming statements on different lines is that a string literal may not span several lines.

Again, there are no fixed rules on the use of spaces and multiple-line statements, just some rules of thumb:

- The Delphi editor and many others have a vertical line you can place after 60 or 70 characters. If you use this line and try to avoid surpassing this limit, your source code will look better when you print it on paper. Otherwise long lines may get broken at any position when you print them.

- When a function or procedure has several parameters, it is common practice to place the parameters on different lines.

- You can leave a line completely white (blank) before a comment or to divide a long piece of code in smaller portions. Even this simple idea can improve the readability of the code, both on screen and when you print it.

- Use spaces to separate the parameters of a function call, and maybe even a space before the initial open parenthesis. Also keep operands of an expression separated. I know that some programmers will disagree with these ideas, but I insist: Spaces are free; you don't pay for them.

Pretty-Printing

The last suggestion on the use of white spaces relates to the typical Pascal language-formatting style, known as pretty-printing. This rule is simple: Each time you need to write a compound statement, indent it two spaces (not a tab, like a C programmer would generally do!) to the right of the current statement. A compound statement inside another compound statement is indented four spaces, and so on:

```
if ... then
  statement;

if ... then
begin
  statement1;
  statement2;
end;
```

```
if ... then
begin
  if ... then
    statement1;
  statement2;
end;
```

The above formatting is based on pretty-printing, but programmers have different interpretations of this general rule. Some programmers indent the begin and end statements to the level of the inner code, some of them indent begin and end and then indent the internal code once more, other programmers put the begin in the line of the if condition (in a C-like fashion). This is mostly a matter of personal taste.

There are Delphi add-in programs you can use to convert an existing source code to the indentation format you prefer. A similar indentation format is often used for lists of variables or data types:

```
type
  Letters = set of Char;

var
  Name: string;
```

Indentation is also used for statements that continue from the previous line:

```
MessageDlg ('This is a message',
  mtInformation, [mbOk], 0);
```

Of course, any such convention is just a suggestion to make the code more readable to other programmers, and it is completely ignored by the compiler. I've tried to use this rule consistently in all of the samples and code fragments in this book. Delphi source code, manuals, and Help examples use a similar formatting style.

Syntax Highlighting

To make it easier to read and write Pascal code, the Delphi editor and many others have a feature called color syntax highlighting. Depending on the meaning in Pascal of the words you type in the editor, they are displayed using different colors. By default, keywords are in bold, strings and comments are in color (and often in italic), and so on.

Reserved words, comments, and strings are probably the three elements that benefit most from this feature. You can see at a glance a misspelled keyword, a string not properly terminated, and the length of a multiple-line comment.

In Delphi, you can easily customize the syntax highlight settings using the Editor Colors page of the Environment Options dialog box. If you are the only person using your computer to look to Pascal source code, choose the colors you like. If you work closely with other programmers, you should all agree on a standard color scheme. I find that working on a computer with a different syntax coloring than the one I am used to is really difficult.

Error Insight and Coding Helpers

Recent versions of the Delphi editor have many more features to help you write correct code. The most obvious is Error Insight, that places a red squiggle under source code elements it doesn't understand in the same fashion a word processor marks spelling mistakes.

Other features, like Code Completion, help you write code by providing a list of legal symbols in the place where you are writing. However, these are editor specific features that I don't want to delve into in detail, as I want to remain focused on the language and not discuss the Delphi editor (even if the Delphi editor is one of the most common tools used for writing Pascal code).

Language Statements

Once you have defined some identifiers, you can use them in statements and in the expressions that are part of some statements. Pascal offers several statements and expressions. Let's look at keywords, expressions, and operators first.

Keywords

Keywords are all the identifiers reserved by the Pascal (or Object Pascal) language. These are symbols that have a predefined meaning and role. Delphi's Help distinguishes between reserved words and directives: Reserved words cannot be used as identifiers, while directives should not be used as such, even if the compiler will accept them. In practice, you should not use any keyword as an identifier.

The following is a complete list of the identifiers, including keywords and other reserved words. Some of them have multiple meanings, some are commonly used, other rather obscure. Even if you are an experienced Delphi programmer you might find one or two you've never heard about. Look them up in the help!

absolute	abstract	and
array	as	asm
assembler	at	automated
begin	case	cdecl
class	const	constructor
contains	default	destructor
dispid	dispinterface	div
do	downto	dynamic
else	end	except
export	exports	external
far	file	finalization
finally	for	forward
function	goto	if
implementation	implements	in
index	inherited	initialization
inline	interface	is
label	library	message
mod	name	near
nil	nodefault	not
object	of	on
or	out	overload
override	package	packed
pascal	private	procedure
program	property	protected
public	published	raise
read	readonly	record
register	reintroduce	repeat
requires	resident	resourcestring
safecall	set	shl
shr	stdcall	stored
string	then	threadvar

```
to            try            type
unit          until          uses
var           virtual        while
with          write          writeonly
xor
```

FreePascal has a few extra reserved words[7]:

```
dispose       exit           false
new           true
```

Literal Values

A literal value is a value you type directly in the program source code. If you need a number with the value of two, you simply enter:

```
2
```

This will be the literal value for an integer number. If you want the same value but for a floating point literal value, you generally add an empty decimal after it:

```
2.0
```

Literal values are not limited to numbers. You can also have characters and strings. Both use single quotes:

```
// literal characters
'K'

// literal string
'Marco'
```

You can also indicate characters by their ASCII number, prefixing the number with the # symbol, as I'll show in more details in the section about the Char data type in the next chapter.

In case you need to have a quote within a string, you'll have to double it. So if I want to have my first and last name (spelled with a final quote rather than an accent) I can write:

```
'Marco Cantu'''
```

---

7   Source: http://www.freepascal.org/docs-html/ref/refsu3.html.

The two quotes stand for a quote within the string, while the third consecutive quote marks the end of the string. Also note that a string literal must be written on a single line.

Expressions and Operators

There isn't a general rule for building expressions, since they mainly depend on the operators being used, and Pascal has a number of operators. There are logical, arithmetic, Boolean, relational, and set operators, plus some others:

```
// sample expressions
20 * 5
30 + n
a < b
c = 10
```

Expressions are common to most programming languages. An expression is any valid combination of constants, variables, literal values, operators, and function results. Expressions can be used to determine the value to assign to a variable, to compute the parameter of a function or procedure, or to test for a condition. Every time you are performing an operation on the value of an identifier, rather than using an identifier by itself, you are using an expression.

Showing the Result of an Expression (a First Program)

If you want to make a few experiments with expressions, there is nothing better than writing a simple program. As for most demos of this book, create a console application, and use writeln function statements to display something on the console output screen[8]. At the end of the program, it is

---

8   In Pascal parameters passed to a function or procedures are enclosed in parenthesis. Some other languages (notably Rebol and Ruby) let you pass parameters simply by writing them after the function or procedure name.

common to add a `readln` function call, so that the program will wait until you press the Enter key, and not close immediately, in which case you might not see the output.

Here is the complete program of the demo program, EPExpressions:

```
program EPExpressions;

{$APPTYPE CONSOLE}

begin
  writeln (20 * 5);
  writeln (30 + 222);
  writeln (3 < 30);
  writeln (12 = 10);

  readln;
end.
```

From now on I'll generally show only the relevant code, skipping some of the details like the `readln` call and the `APPTYPE` directive. The source code examples available with the book will have complete and running programs, though. This is the output of the program:

```
100
252
TRUE
FALSE
```

Operators and Precedence

If you have ever written a program in your life, you already know what an expression is, as they constitute the base building blocks of any programming language. Here, I'll highlight specific elements of Pascal operators. You can see a list of the operators of the language below, grouped by precedence:

Unary Operators (Highest Precedence)

@	Address of variable or function (returns a pointer)
not	Boolean or bitwise not

Multiplicative and Bitwise Operators

*	Arithmetic multiplication or set intersection
/	Floating-point division
div	Integer division

mod	Modulus (the remainder of integer division)
as	Allows a type-checked conversion at runtime
and	Boolean or bitwise and
shl	Bitwise left shift
shr	Bitwise right shift

Additive Operators

+	Arithmetic addition, set union, string concatenation, pointer offset addition
-	Arithmetic subtraction, set difference, pointer offset subtraction
or	Boolean or bitwise or
xor	Boolean or bitwise exclusive or

Relational and Comparison Operators (Lowest Precedence)

=	Test whether equal
<>	Test whether not equal
<	Test whether less than
>	Test whether greater than
<=	Test whether less than or equal to, or a subset of a set
>=	Test whether greater than or equal to, or a superset of a set
in	Test whether the item is a member of the set
is	Test whether object is compatible with a specified type definition (which is only of use in object oriented programming.)

Contrary to most other programming languages, the and and or operators have higher precedence than comparison ones. So if you write:

```
a < b and c < d
```

the compiler will do the and operation first, resulting in a compiler error. So you should enclose each of the < expressions in parentheses:

```
(a < b) and (c < d)
```

Some of the common operators have different meanings when used with different data types. For example, the + operator can be used to add two numbers, concatenate two strings, make the union of two sets, and even add an offset to a PChar pointer. However, you cannot add two characters, as is possible in C.

Another unusual operator is div. In Pascal, you can divide any two numbers (real or integers) with the / operator, and you'll invariably get a real-number result. If you need to divide two integers and want an integer result, use the div operator instead. Here are two sample assignments (this code will become clearer as we cover data types in the next chapter):

```
realVal := 123 / 12;
intergerVal := 123 div 12;
```

Set Operators

The set operators include union (+), difference (-), intersection (*), membership test (in), plus some relational operators. To add an element to a set, you can make the union of the set with another one that has only the elements you need. Here's a Delphi example related to font styles:

```
Style := Style + [fsBold];
Style := Style + [fsBold, fsItalic] - [fsUnderline];
```

As an alternative, you can use the standard Include and Exclude procedures, which are much more efficient (but cannot be used with component properties of the set type):

```
Include (Style, fsBold);
```

Conclusion

Now that we know the basic layout of a Pascal program, we are ready to start exploring its meaning. We'll start by looking at predefined and user defined data types, then we'll start using keywords to form programming statements.

Chapter 3: Types, Variables, And Constants

The original Pascal language introduced some new notions, which have now become quite common in programming languages. The first then revolutionary notion is that of *data type*. The type determines the values a variable can hold, and the operations that can be performed on it.

The concept of type is stronger in Pascal than in C, where the arithmetic data types are almost interchangeable, and much stronger than in the original versions of BASIC, which had no similar concept. That's why programmers refer to Pascal as a *strongly-typed* language.

Marco Cantù, Essential Pascal

Variables

Pascal requires all variables to be declared before they are used. Every time you declare a variable, you must specify a data type. Here are some sample variable declarations:

```
var
  Value: Integer;
  IsCorrect: Boolean;
  A, B: Char;
```

The var keyword can be used in several places in a program, such as at the beginning of a function or procedure, to declare variables local to a routine, or inside a unit to declare global variables. After the var keyword comes a list of variable names, followed by a colon and the name of the data type. You can write more than one variable name on a single line, as A and B in the last statement of the previous code snippet.

Once you have defined a variable of a given type, you can only perform the operations supported by its data type on it. For example, you can use the Boolean value in a test and the integer value in a numerical expression. You cannot mix Booleans and integers (as you can with the C language).

Using simple assignments, we can write the following code (which is part of the Variables example[9]):

```
Value := 10;
IsCorrect := True;
```

Given the previous variable declarations, these two assignments are correct. The next statement, instead, is not correct, as the two variables have different data types:

```
Value := IsCorrect; // error
```

If you try to compile this code, the compiler issues an error with a description like this:

```
[DCC Error]: Incompatible types: 'Integer' and 'Boolean'
```

Usually, errors like these are programming errors, because it does not make sense to assign a True or False value to a variable of the Integer data type. You should not blame the compiler for these errors. It only warns you that there is something wrong in your code.

---

9   The EPVariables example has the variable declarations and the assignments listed in this section, plus a couple of writeln statements to display something on screen.

Of course, it is often possible to convert the value of a variable from one type to another type. In some cases, the conversion is automatic, but usually you need to call a specific system function that changes the internal representation of the data.

In Pascal, you can assign an initial value to a global variable while you declare it. For example, you can write:

```
var
  Value: Integer = 10;
  Correct: Boolean = True;
```

This initialization technique works only for global variables, not for variables declared inside a procedure or function.

Constants

Pascal also allows the declaration of constants allowing you to give meaningful names to values that do not change during program execution. To declare a constant you don't need to specify a data type, but only assign an initial value. The compiler will look at the value and automatically use its proper data type. Here are some sample declarations (from the EPConstants example):

```
const
  Thousand = 1000;
  Pi = 3.14;
  AuthorName = 'Marco Cantu';
```

Pascal determines the constant data type based on its value. In the example above, the `Thousand` constant is assumed to be of type `SmallInt`, the smallest integral type which can hold it. If you want to tell Pascal to use a specific type you can simply add the type name in the declaration, as in:

```
const
  Thousand: Integer = 1000;
```

When you declare a constant, the compiler can choose whether to assign a memory location to the constant, and save its value there, or to duplicate the actual value each time the constant is used. This second approach makes sense particularly for simple constants.

Like Turbo Pascal, the 16-bit version of Delphi allowed you to change the value of a typed constant at run-time, as if it was a variable. The 32-bit versions still permits this behavior for backward compatibility when you enable the $J compiler directive, or use the corresponding *Assignable typed constants* check box of the Compiler page of the Project Options dialog box. This setting was on by default until Delphi 6, but in any case you are strongly advised not to use this trick as a general programming technique. Assigning a new value to a constant disables all the compiler optimizations on constants. In such a case, simply declare a variable instead.

Resource String Constants

When you define a string constant, instead of writing a standard constant declaration you can use a specific directive, resourcestring, that indicates to the compiler and linker to treat the string like a Windows resource:

```
const
   sAuthorName = 'Marco';

resourcestring
   strAuthorName = 'Marco';
```

In both cases you are defining a constant; that is, a value you don't change during program execution. The difference is only in the implementation. A string constant defined with the resourcestring directive is stored in the resources of the program, in a string table.

To see this capability in action, you can look at the EPConstants example, which includes the following code:

```
resourcestring
   strAuthorName = 'Marco Cantù';
   strBookName = 'Essential Pascal';

begin
   writeln (strBookName + ' ' + strAuthorName);
```

The output of the two strings appears with a space in between. The interesting aspect of this program is that if you examine it with a resource explorer (there is one available among the examples that ship with Delphi) you'll see the new strings in the resources. This means that the strings are not part of the compiled code, but stored in a separate area of the executable file (the EXE file)[10].

In short, the advantages of using resources are more efficient memory handling performed by Windows and a better way of localizing a program (translating the strings to a different language) without having to modify its source code. As a rule of thumb, you should use `resourcestring` for any text that is shown to users and might need translating, and internal constants for every other internal program string, like a configuration file name.

Data Types

In Pascal there are several predefined data types, which can be divided into three groups: *ordinal types*, *real types*, and *strings*. We'll discuss ordinal and real types in the following sections, while strings are covered later in this chapter[11].

Delphi also includes a *non-typed* data type, called *variant*, discussed in Chapter 10. Strangely enough a variant is a type without proper type-checking. It was introduced in Delphi 2 to handle Windows OLE Automation, but found its way to other areas of the Delphi libraries.

Ordinal Types

Ordinal types are based on the concept of order or sequence. Not only can you compare two values to see which is higher, but you can also ask for the next or previous values of any value and compute the lowest and highest possible values.

The three most important predefined ordinal types are `Integer`, `Boolean`, and `Char` (character). However, there are other related types that have the same meaning but a different internal representation and support a different

---

10 Although this might sound odd, resource strings are available also on Kylix.

11 I'll also introduce some types defined by the Delphi libraries (not predefined by the compiler), which can be considered as predefined types for all practical purposes.

range of values. The following table lists the ordinal data types used for representing numbers:

Size	Signed	Unsigned
8 bits	ShortInt: -128 to 127	Byte: 0 to 255
16 bits	SmallInt: -32768 to 32767	Word: 0 to 65,535
16/32 bits	Integer	Cardinal
32 bits	LongInt: -2,147,483,648 to 2,147,483,647	LongWord: 0 to 4,294,967,295
64 bits	Int64: -9223372036854775808 to 9223372036854775807	

As you can see, these types correspond to different representations of numbers, depending on the number of bits used to express the value, and the presence or absence of a sign bit. Signed values can be positive or negative, but have a smaller range of values, because one less bit is available for the value itself. You can refer to the Range example, discussed in the next section, for the actual range of values of each type.

The last group (marked as 16/32) indicates values having a different representation in the 16-bit and 32-bit versions of Delphi. Integer and Cardinal are frequently used, because they correspond to the native representation of numbers in the CPU. I'll explain the benefits of using Integer and Cardinal later.

Integer Types

In Delphi 2 and 3, the 32-bit unsigned numbers indicated by the Cardinal type were actually 31-bit values, with a range up to 2 gigabytes. Delphi 4 introduced a new unsigned numeric type, LongWord, which uses a truly 32-bit value up to 4 gigabytes. The Cardinal type is now an alias of the LongWord type. LongWord permits 2GB more data to be addressed by an unsigned number, as mentioned above. Moreover, it corresponds to the native representation of numbers in the CPU.

Another new type introduced in Delphi 4 is the Int64 type, which represents integer numbers with up to 18 digits. This new type is fully supported by some of the ordinal type routines (such as `High` and `Low`), numeric routines (such as `Inc` and `Dec`), and string-conversion routines (such as `IntToStr`).[12]

Boolean

Boolean values other than the `Boolean` type are seldom used. Some Boolean values with specific representations are required by Windows API functions (and COM libraries). The types are `ByteBool`, `WordBool`, and `LongBool`.

In Delphi 3 for compatibility with Visual Basic and OLE automation, the data types `ByteBool`, `WordBool`, and `LongBool` were modified to represent the value True with -1, while the value False is still 0. The `Boolean` data type remains unchanged (True is 1, False is 0), although the actual numeric values should be irrelevant and should not be abused (like in C).

Characters

Finally there are two different representation for characters: `ANSIChar` and `WideChar`. The first type represents 8-bit characters, corresponding to the ANSI character set traditionally used by Windows; the second represents 16-bit characters, corresponding to the new Unicode characters supported (alongside with the traditional ones) by recent versions of Windows.

Most of the time you'll simply use the `Char` type, which from Delphi 3 to Delphi 2007 corresponds to `ANSIChar`. Keep in mind, anyway, that the first 256 Unicode characters correspond exactly to the ANSI characters.

Constant characters can be represented with their symbolic notation, as in `'k'`, or with a numeric notation, as in `#78`. The latter can also be expressed using the `Chr` function, as in `Chr (78)`. The opposite conversion can be done with the `Ord` function. It is generally better to use the symbolic notation when indicating letters, digits, or symbols.

When referring to special characters, like those below `#32`, you'll generally use the numeric notation. The following list includes some of the most commonly used special characters:

---

12 There are also functions which can convert strings to these 64 bit integers. I'll cover moving data from strings to integers and vice versa later in the book.

#8	backspace
#9	tabulator
#10	newline
#13	carriage return
#27	escape

Displaying Ordinal Ranges

To give you an idea of the different ranges of some of the ordinal types, I've written a simple Delphi program named EPRange. The EPRange program displays the name, size, and range of some data types, separating the values belonging to the same data type with tabulators:

```
program EPRange;

{$APPTYPE CONSOLE}

begin
  write ('Integer');
  write (#9);
  write (SizeOf (Integer));
  write (#9);
  write (Low (Integer));
  write (#9);
  write (High (Integer));
  writeln;

  write ('SmallInt');
  write (#9);
  write (SizeOf (SmallInt));
  write (#9);
  write (Low (SmallInt));
  write (#9);
  write (High (SmallInt));
  writeln;

  write ('Int64');
  write (#9);
  write (SizeOf (Int64));
  write (#9);
  write (Low (Int64));
  write (#9);
  write (High (Int64));
  writeln;
```

```
write ('Char');
write (#9);
write (SizeOf (Char));
write (#9);
write (Ord(Low (Char)));
write (#9);
write (Ord(High (Char)));
writeln;

readln;
end.
```

The code is somewhat repetitive, and it could have been written in a much nicer way[13], but I didn't want to introduce too many concepts at once.

This is the output (slightly reformatted for clarity):

```
Integer    4      -2147483648 2147483647
SmallInt   2      -32768         32767
Int64      8      -9223372036854775808
                               9223372036854775807
Char       1      0              255
```

The program uses three functions: SizeOf, High, and Low. The result of the SizeOf function is an integer indicating the number of bytes required to represent values of the given type.

The results of the last two functions are ordinals of the same type as that of the value supplied to them, indicating the valid range of values represented by the type itself. To display the range of the Char type, the program converts the character into its numeric representation, using Ord, as character #0 is non-printable and character #255 is a white space.

The size of the Integer type varies depending on the CPU and operating system you are using. In 16-bit Windows (that is, using Delphi 1 for example), an Integer variable is two bytes wide. In 32-bit Windows (including all later versions of Delphi, until now), an Integer is four bytes wide.

The different representations of the Integer type are not a problem, as long as your program doesn't make any assumptions about the size of integers. If you happen to save an Integer to a file using one version and retrieve it with another, though, you're going to have some trouble. In this situation,

---

13 Delphi has a rich support for Run Time Type Information (RTTI) you can use to operated on directly on data types at runtime, but this topic, as you can probably guess, is quite advanced and way outside of the scope of this book..

you should choose a platform-independent data type (such as `LongInt`, `SmallInt`, or `Int64`).

For mathematical computation or generic code, your best bet is to stick with the standard integer representation for the specific platform--that is, use the `Integer` type--because this is what the CPU likes best.

The `Integer` type should be your first choice when handling integer numbers. Use a different representation only when there is a compelling reason to do so.

Ordinal Types Routines

There are some system routines (routines defined in the Pascal language and in the Delphi system unit) that work on ordinal types. They are shown in the following table:

`Dec`	Decrements the variable passed as parameter, by one or by the value of the optional second parameter.
`Inc`	Increments the variable passed as parameter, by one or by the specified value[14].
`Odd`	Returns True if the argument is an odd number.
`Pred`	Returns the value before the argument in the order determined by the data type, the predecessor.
`Succ`	Returns the value after the argument, the successor.
`Ord`	Returns a number indicating the order of the argument within the set of values of the data type.
`Low`	Returns the lowest value in the range of the ordinal type passed as its parameter.
`High`	Returns the highest value in the range of the ordinal data type.

Notice that some of these routines, when applied to constants, are automatically evaluated by the compiler and replaced with their value. For example, if

---

14 C++ programmers should notice that the two versions of the `Inc` procedure, with one or two parameters, correspond to the ++ and += operators (the same holds for the `Dec` procedure).

you call High(X) where X is defined as an Integer, the compiler replaces the expression with the highest possible value of the Integer data type.

Real Types

Real types represent floating-point numbers in various formats. Here is a list of floating-point data types:

Single   The smallest storage size is given by Single numbers, which are implemented with a 4-byte value.

Double   These are floating-point numbers implemented with 8 bytes.

Extended   These are numbers implemented with 10 bytes.

These are all floating-point data types with different precision, which correspond to the IEEE standard floating-point representations, and are directly supported by the CPU, for maximum speed.

In Delphi 2 and Delphi 3 the Real type had the same definition as in the 16-bit version; it was a 48-bit type. But its usage was deprecated by Borland, who suggested that you use the Single, Double, and Extended types instead. The reason for their suggestion is that the old 6-byte format is neither supported by the Intel CPU nor listed among the official IEEE real types. To completely overcome the problem, Delphi 4 modified the definition of the Real type to represent a standard 8-byte (64-bit) floating-point number[15].

In addition to the advantage of using a standard definition, this change allows components to publish properties based on the Real type, something Delphi 3 did not allow. Among the disadvantages there might be compatibility problems. If necessary, you can overcome the possibility of incompatibility by sticking to the Delphi 2 and 3 definition of the type; do this by using the following compiler option:

```
{$REALCOMPATIBILITY ON}
```

There are also two strange non-ordinal data types[16]:

---

15 A new type called Real48 was introduced for backward compatibility with the Real type of older Borland Pascal compilers.

Comp   describes very big integers using 8 bytes (which can hold numbers with 18 decimal digits)

Currency   (not available in 16-bit Delphi) indicates a fixed-point decimal value with four decimal digits, and the same 64-bit representation as the Comp type. As the name implies, the Currency data type has been added to handle very precise monetary values, with four decimal places.

We cannot build a program similar to the EPRange example with real data types, because we cannot use the High and Low functions or the Ord function on real-type variables. Real types represent (in theory) an infinite set of numbers; ordinal types represent a fixed set of values.

Let me explain this better. when you have the integer 23 you can determine which is the following value. Integers are finite (they have a determined range and they have an order). Floating point numbers are infinite even within a small range, and have no order: in fact, how many values are there between 23 and 24? And which number follows 23.46? Is it 23.47, 23.461, or 23.4601? That's really impossible to know!

For this reason, whilst it makes sense to ask for the ordinal position of the character 'w' in the range of the Char data type, it makes no sense at all to ask the same question about 7143.1562 in the range of a floating-point data type. Although you can indeed know whether one real number has a higher value than another, it makes no sense to ask how many real numbers exist before a given number (this is the meaning of the Ord function).

Real types have a limited role in the user interface portion of the code (the Windows side), but they are fully supported by Delphi, including the database side. The support of IEEE standard floating-point types makes the Object Pascal language completely appropriate for the wide range of programs that require numerical computations. If you are interested in this aspect, you can look at the arithmetic functions provided by the compiler's system unit (see the compiler documentation or use the help system for more details).

Delphi and FreePascal also have a Math unit that defines advanced mathematical routines, covering trigonometric functions (such as the ArcCosh function), finance (such as the InterestPayment function), and statistics

---

16 Both FreePascal and GNU Pascal include the Comp data type. It is correctly considered an Integer type in GNU Pascal. FreePascal includes the Currency data type.

(such as the `MeanAndStdDev` procedure). There are a number of these routines, some of which sound quite strange to me, such as the `MomentSkew-Kurtosis` function (I'll let you find out what this is).

Date and Time

Pascal implementations typically use floating-point data types to handle date and time information. To be more precise both Delphi and FreePascal define a specific `TDateTime` data type[17].

These are a floating-point type, because the type must be wide enough to store years, months, days, hours, minutes, and seconds, down to millisecond resolution in a single variable. Dates are stored as the number of days since 1899-12-30[18] (with negative values indicating dates before 1899) in the integer part of the `TDateTime` value. Times are stored as fractions of a day in the decimal part of the value.

`TDateTime` is not a predefined type the compiler understands, but it is defined in the system unit as:

```
type
  TDateTime = type Double;
```

Using the `TDateTime` type is quite easy, because Delphi includes a number of functions that operate on this type. Here you can find a list with some of these functions:

Now	Returns the current date and time into a date/time value.
Date	Returns only the current date.
Time	Returns only the current time.

---

17 GNU Pascal adopts a different approach to storing dates and times. It defines a `TimeStamp` record (more about records later) which stores each element of the date and time separately. It has a comparatively limited number of routines for handling dates and times as individual elements of the date and time, such as Hour, can be directly accessed. Whilst this approach is simpler and slightly faster, the penalty for using it is that it uses much, much more memory.

18 Delphi 1.0 used a different zero-point for `TDateTime` values.

Marco Cantù, Essential Pascal

DateTimeToStr	Converts a date and time value into a string, using default formatting; to have more control on the conversion use the FormatDateTime function instead.
DateTimeToString	Copies the date and time values into a string buffer, with default formatting.
DateToStr	Converts the date portion of a date/time value into a string.
TimeToStr	Converts the time portion of a date/time value into a string.
FormatDateTime	Formats a date and time using the specified format; you can specify which values you want to see and which format to use by providing a complex format string.
StrToDateTime	Converts a string with date and time information to a date/time value, raising an exception in case of an error in the format of the string. Its companion function, StrToDateTimeDef returns the default value in case of an error rather than raising an exception.
StrToDate	Converts a string representing a date into a date/time value.
StrToTime	Converts a string representing a time into a date/time value.
DayOfWeek	Returns the number corresponding to the day of the week of the date/time value passed as parameter.
DecodeDate	Retrieves the year, month, and day values from a date value.
DecodeTime	Retrieves the hours, minutes, seconds, and milliseconds from a date value.
EncodeDate	Turns year, month, and day values into a date/time value.
EncodeTime	Turns hour, minute, second, and millisecond values into a date/time value.

To show you how to use this data type and some of its related routines, I've built a simple example, named TimeNow. When the program starts it automatically computes and displays the current time and date.

Marco Cantù, Essential Pascal

```
StartTime := Now;
writeln (TimeToStr (StartTime));
writeln (DateToStr (StartTime));
```

The first statement is a call to the Now function, which returns the current date and time. This value is stored in the StartTime variable, declared as a global variable as follows:

```
var
   StartTime: TDateTime;
```

The next two statements display the time portion of the TDateTime value, converted into a string, and the date portion of the same value. This is the output of the program:

```
6:33:14 PM
10/7/2007
```

To compile this program you need to refer to functions that are part of a commonly used Pascal unit (a source code file), called SysUtils. To accomplish this you have to write[19]:

```
uses
   SysUtils;
```

Besides calling TimeToStr and DateToStr you can use the more powerful FormatDateTime function, as I've done in the last method above (see the Help file or documentation for details on the formatting parameters).

Notice that time and date values are transformed into strings depending on the system's international settings. The runtime reads these values from the system and copies them to a number of global variables declared in the SysUtils unit. Some of them are:

```
DateSeparator: Char;
ShortDateFormat: string;
LongDateFormat: string;
TimeSeparator: Char;
TimeAMString: string;
TimePMString: string;
ShortTimeFormat: string;
LongTimeFormat: string;
ShortMonthNames: array [1..12] of string;
LongMonthNames: array [1..12] of string;
ShortDayNames: array [1..7] of string;
LongDayNames: array [1..7] of string;
```

---

19 Units and uses statements are covered in detail in Chapter 11.

More global variables relate to currency and floating-point number formatting. You can find the complete list in the Help file or documentation.

Specific Windows Types

The predefined data types we have seen so far are part of the Pascal language. Delphi and FreePascal also include other data types defined by Windows. These data types are not an integral part of the language, but they are part of the Windows libraries. Windows types include new common types (such as DWORD or UINT), many records (or structures), several pointer types, and so on.

Among Windows data types, the most important type is represented by handles, discussed in Chapter 9.

Typecasting and Type Conversions

As we have seen, you cannot assign a variable to one of a different type. When you need to do this, there are two choices.

The first choice is *typecasting*, which uses a simple functional notation, with the name of the destination data type:

```
var
  N: Integer;
  C: Char;
  B: Boolean;

begin
  N := Integer ('x');
  C := Char (N);
  B := Boolean (0);
```

You can typecast between data types having the same size. It is usually safe to typecast between ordinal types, or between real types, but you can also typecast between pointer types (and also objects) as long as you know what you are doing.

Casting, however, is generally a dangerous programming practice, because it allows you to access a value as if it represented something else. Since the internal representations of data types generally do not match, you risk accidentally creating hard-to-track errors. For this reason, you should generally avoid typecasting.

The second choice is to use a type-conversion routine. The routines for the various types of conversions are summarized in the following list:

Chr	Converts an ordinal number into an ANSI character.
Ord	Converts an ordinal-type value into the number indicating its order.
Round	Converts a real-type value into an Integer-type value, rounding its value.
Trunc	Converts a real-type value into an Integer-type value, truncating its value.
Int	Returns the Integer part of the floating-point value argument.
IntToStr	Converts a number into a string.
IntToHex	Converts a number into a string with its hexadecimal representation.
StrToInt	Converts a string into a number, raising an exception if the string does not represent a valid integer.
StrToIntDef	Converts a string into a number, using a default value if the string is not correct.
Val	Converts a string into a number (traditional Turbo Pascal routine, available for compatibility).
Str	Converts a number into a string, using formatting parameters (traditional Turbo Pascal routine, available for compatibility).
StrPas	Converts a null-terminated string into a Pascal-style string. This conversion is automatically done for AnsiStrings in 32-bit Delphi. (See the section on strings later in this chapter.)
StrPCopy	Copies a Pascal-style string into a null-terminated string. This conversion is done with a simple PChar

	cast in 32-bit Delphi. (See the section on strings later in this chapter.)
StrPLCopy	Copies a portion of a Pascal-style string into a null-terminated string.
FloatToDecimal	Converts a floating-point value to record including its decimal representation (exponent, digits, sign).
FloatToStr	Converts a floating-point value to its string representation using default formatting.
FloatToStrF	Converts a floating-point value to its string representation using the specified formatting.
FloatToText	Copies a floating-point value to a string buffer, using the specified formatting.
FloatToTextFmt	As the previous one, copies the floating-point value to a string buffer, using the specified formatting.
StrToFloat	Converts a Pascal string to a floating-point value.
TextToFloat	Converts a null-terminated string to a floating-point value.

Some of these routines work on the data types that we'll discuss in the following sections. Notice that the table doesn't include routines for special types (such as TDateTime or variant) or routines specifically intended for formatting, like the powerful Format and FormatFloat routines.

In recent versions of Delphi's Pascal compiler[20], the Round function is based on the native implementation offered by the CPU. This processor adopts the so-called "Banker's Rounding", which rounds middle values (such as 5.5 or 6.5) up and down depending whether they follow an odd or an even number.

Summary

In this chapter we explored the basic notion of type in Pascal. But the language has another very important feature: It allows programmers to define new custom data types, called user-defined data types, which are covered in the next chapter.

---

20 And in the FreePascal Compiler

Chapter 4: User-Defined Data Types

Along with the notion of type, one of the great new ideas introduced by the Pascal language was the ability to define new data types in a program. Programmers can define their own data types by means of *type definitions*, such as subrange types, array types, record types, enumerated types, pointer types, and set types. The most important user-defined data type is the class, which is part of the object-oriented extensions of Object Pascal, not covered in this book.

If you think that type constructors are common in many programming languages, you are right, but Pascal was the first language to introduce the idea in a formal and very precise way.

Named and Unnamed Types

User-defined data types can be given a name for later use or applied to a variable directly. The convention in Delphi is to use a letter T prefix to denote any data type, including classes but not limited to them. I strongly suggest you to stick to this rule, even if might not feel natural at first.

When you give a name to a type, you must provide a specific section in the code, such as the following:

```
type
  // subrange definition
  TUppercase = 'A'..'Z';

  // array definition
  TDayTemperatures = array [1..24] of Integer;

  // record definition
  TMyDate = record
    Month: Byte;
    Day: Byte;
    Year: Integer;
  end;

  // enumerated type definition
  TColors = (Red, Yellow, Green, Cyan, Blue, Violet);

  // set definition
  TLetters = set of Char;
```

Similar type definitions can be used directly to define a variable without an explicit type name, as in the following code:

```
var
  DecemberTemperature: array [1..31] of Byte;
  ColorCode: array [Red..Violet] of Word;
  Palette: set of Colors;
```

In general, you should avoid using *unnamed* types as in the code above, because you cannot pass them as parameters to routines or declare other variables of the same type.

The *type compatibility rules* of Pascal, in fact, are based on type names, not on the actual definition of the types. Two variables of two identical types are still not compatible, unless their types have exactly the same name, and unnamed types are given internal names by the compiler. Get used to defining a data type each time you need a variable with a complicated structure, and you won't regret the time you've spent doing it.

But what do these type definitions mean? I'll provide some descriptions for those who are not familiar with Pascal type constructs. I'll also try to underline the differences from the same constructs in other programming languages, so you might be interested in reading the following sections even if you are familiar with the kind of type definitions listed above. Finally, I'll show some examples and introduce some tools that will allow you to access type information dynamically.

Subrange Types

A subrange type defines a range of values within the range of another type (hence the name *subrange*). For example, you can define a subrange of the Integer type, from 1 to 10 or from 100 to 1000, or you can define a subrange of the Char type with uppercase characters only, as in:

```
type
  TTen = 1..10;
  TOverHundred = 100..1000;
  TUppercase = 'A'..'Z';
```

In the definition of a subrange, you don't need to specify the name of the base type. You just need to supply two constants of that type. The original type must be an ordinal type, and the resulting type will be another ordinal type. When you have defined a variable as a subrange, you can then assign it any value within that range. This code is valid:

```
var
  UppLetter: TUpperCase;

begin
  UppLetter := 'F';
```

But this one is not:

```
var
  UppLetter: TUpperCase;

begin
  UppLetter := 'e'; // compile-time error
```

Writing the code above results in a compile-time error, *"Constant expression violates subrange bounds."* If you write the following code instead:

```
var
  UppLetter: TUppercase;
  Letter: Char;

begin
  Letter := 'e';
  UppLetter := Letter;
```

Delphi will compile it. At run-time, if you have enabled the Range Checking compiler option (in the Compiler page of the Project Options dialog box), you'll get a *Range check error* message.

I suggest that you turn on this compiler option while you are developing a program, so it'll be more robust and easier to debug, as in case of errors you'll get an explicit message and not an undetermined behavior. You can eventually disable this option for the final build of the program, so that it will run a little faster. However, the increase in speed is so little that I suggest you leave all these run-time checks turned on, even when a shipping program. The same holds true for other run-time checking options, such as overflow and stack checking.

Enumerated Types

Enumerated types (usually referred to as "enums") constitute another user-defined ordinal type. Instead of indicating a range of an existing type, in an enumeration you list all of the possible values for the type. In other words, an enumeration is a list of values. Here are some examples:

```
type
  TColors = (Red, Yellow, Green, Cyan, Blue, Violet);
  TSuit = (Club, Diamond, Heart, Spade);
```

Each value in the list has an associated *ordinality*, starting with zero. When you apply the Ord function to a value of an enumerated type, you get this "zero-based" value. For example, Ord (Diamond) returns 1.

Enumerated types can have different internal representations. By default, Delphi uses an 8-bit representation, unless there are more than 256 different values, in which case it uses the 16-bit representation. There is also a 32-bit representation, which might be useful for compatibility with C or C++ libraries[21].

The Delphi VCL (Visual Component Library) uses enumerated types in many places. For example, the style of the border of a form is defined as follows[22]:

```
type
  TFormBorderStyle = (bsNone, bsSingle, bsSizeable,
    bsDialog, bsSizeToolWin, bsToolWindow);
```

Set Types

Set types indicate a group of values, where the list of available values is indicated by the ordinal type the set is based onto. These ordinal types are usually limited, and quite often represented by an enumeration or a subrange. If we take the subrange 1..3, the possible values of the set based on it include only 1, only 2, only 3, both 1 and 2, both 1 and 3, both 2 and 3, all the three values, or none of them.

A variable usually holds one of the possible values of the range of its type. A set-type variable, instead, can contain none, one, two, three, or more values of the range. It can even include all of the values. Here is an example of a set:

```
type
  TLetters = set of TUppercase;
```

Now I can define a variable of this type and assign to it some values of the original type. To indicate some values in a set, you write a comma-separated list, enclosed within square brackets. The following code shows the assignment to a variable of several values, a single value, and an empty value:

```
var
  Letters1, Letters2, Letters3: TLetters;

begin
  Letters1 := ['A', 'B', 'C'];
  Letters2 := ['K'];
  Letters3 := [];
```

---

21 You can change the default representation of enumerated types, asking for a larger one, by using the $Z compiler directive.

22 When the value of a property is an enumeration, you can choose its value from the list displayed in the Object Inspector.

You can revise the operations you can make on a set (which comprise the Include and Exclude statements) in "Set Operators" section of Chapter 2.

In Pascal, a set is generally used to indicate nonexclusive flags. For example, the following two lines of code (which are part of the Delphi library) declare an enumeration of possible icons for the border of a window and the corresponding set type[23]:

```
type
  TBorderIcon = (biSystemMenu, biMinimize,
    biMaximize, biHelp);
  TBorderIcons = set of TBorderIcon;
```

In fact, a given window might have none of these icons, one of them, or more than one. Another property based on a set type is the style of a font. Possible values indicate a bold, italic, underline, and strike-through font. Of course the same font can be both italic and bold, have no attributes, or have them all. For this reason it is declared as a set. You can assign values to this set in the code of a program as follows:

```
Font.Style := []; // no style
Font.Style := [fsBold]; // bold style only
Font.Style := [fsBold, fsItalic]; // two styles
```

You can also operate on a set in many different ways, including adding two variables of the same set type (or, to be more precise, computing the union of the two set variables):

```
Font.Style := OldStyle + [fsUnderline]; // merge two sets
```

Array Types

Array types define lists of a fixed number of elements of a specific type. You generally use an *index* within square brackets to access one of the elements of the array. Square brackets are also used to specify the possible values of the index when the array is declared. For example, you can define a group of 24 integers with this code:

```
type
  TDayTemperatures = array [1..24] of Integer;
```

---

23 When working with the Object Inspector in Delphi, you can provide the values of a set by expanding the selection (double-click on the property name or click on the plus sign on its left) and toggling on and off the presence of each value.

In the array definition, you need to pass a subrange type within square brackets, or define a new specific subrange type using two constants of an ordinal type. This subrange specifies the valid indexes of the array. Since you specify both the upper and the lower index of the array, the indexes don't need to be zero-based, as is necessary in C, C++, Java, and other languages.

Since the array indexes are based on subranges, Pascal can check their range as we've already seen. An invalid constant subrange results in a compile-time error; and an out-of-range index used at run-time results in a run-time error if the corresponding compiler option is enabled.

Using the array definition above, you can set the value of a DayTemp1 variable of the TDayTemperatures type as follows:

```
type
  TDayTemperatures = array [1..24] of Integer;

var
  DayTemp1: TDayTemperatures;

procedure AssignTemp;
begin
  DayTemp1 [1] := 54;
  DayTemp1 [2] := 52;
  ...
  DayTemp1 [24] := 66;
  DayTemp1 [25] := 67; // compile-time error
```

An array can have more than one dimension, as in the following examples:

```
type
  TMonthTemps = array [1..24, 1..31] of Integer;
  TYearTemps = array [1..24, 1..31, Jan..Dec] of Integer;
```

These two array types are built on the same core types. So you could also declare them using the preceding data types, as in the following code:

```
type
  TMonthTemps = array [1..31] of TDayTemperatures;
  TYearTemps = array [Jan..Dec] of TMonthTemps;
```

This declaration inverts the order of the indexes as presented above, but it also allows assignment of whole blocks between variables. For example, the following statement copies January's temperatures to February:

```
var
  ThisYear: TYearTemps;

begin
  ThisYear[Feb] := ThisYear[Jan];
```

You can also define a *zero-based* array, an array type with the lower bound set to zero. Generally, the use of more logical bounds is an advantage, since you don't need to use the index 2 to access the third item, and so on. Windows, Linux and Mac OS X, however, invariably uses zero-based arrays (because they are based on the C language) and, for this reason Delphi and many other component libraries tend to do the same.

If you need to work on an array, you can always test its bounds by using the standard Low and High functions, which return the lower and upper bounds. Using Low and High when operating on an array is highly recommended, especially in loops, since it makes the code independent of the range of the array. Later, you can change the declared range of the array indexes, and the code that uses Low and High will still work. If you write a loop hard-coding the range of an array you'll have to update the code of the loop when the array size changes. Low and High make your code easier to maintain and more reliable[24].

Pascal uses arrays mainly in the form of array properties. I'll show you some more examples of array properties in the next chapter, when discussing Pascal loops.

Delphi 4 introduced dynamic arrays, arrays that can be resized at runtime allocating the proper amount of memory, into Object Pascal . Using dynamic arrays is easy, but I felt it better to cover them later in the discussion of how Pascal handles memory in Chapter 8.

Record Types

Record types define fixed collections of items of different types. Each element, or *field*, has its own type. The definition of a record type lists all these fields, giving each a name you'll use later to access it.

Here is a small listing with the definition of a record type, the declaration of a variable of that type, and few statements using this variable:

---

24 Incidentally, there is no run-time overhead for using Low and High with arrays. They are resolved at compile-time into constant expressions, not actual function calls. This compile-time resolution of expressions and function calls also happens for many other simple system functions.

```
type
  TMyDate = record
    Year: Integer;
    Month: Byte;
    Day: Byte;
  end;

var
  BirthDay: TMyDate;

begin
  BirthDay.Year := 1997;
  BirthDay.Month := 2;
  BirthDay.Day := 14;
end;
```

Classes and objects can be considered an extension of the record type[25]. Delphi libraries tend to use class types instead of record types, but there are many record types defined by the Windows API.

Record types can also have a variant part; that is, multiple fields can be mapped to the same memory area, even if they have a different data type. (This corresponds to a union in the C language.) Alternatively, you can use these variant fields or groups of fields to access the same memory location within a record, but considering those values from different perspectives. The main uses of this type were to store similar but different data and to obtain an effect similar to that of typecasting (something used in the early days of Pascal, when direct typecasting was not allowed). The use of variant record types has been largely replaced by object-oriented and other modern techniques, although Delphi uses them internally in some special cases.

The use of a variant record type is not type-safe and is not recommended programming practice, particularly for beginners. Expert programmers can indeed use variant record types, and the core of the Delphi libraries makes use of them. You won't need to tackle them until you are really a Delphi expert, anyway.

Before using variant record types, consider also that the .NET version of Delphi doesn't fully support them, as they can be used only in "unsafe" portions of code. These features, in fact, are not considered safe by the .NET runtime (and for a good reason).

---

25 In recent versions of Delphi, records can also have methods (that is, functions associated with them) and support the overloading of language operators. These topics are covered in my "Delphi 2007 Handbook" (see my web site for details).

Pointers

A pointer type defines a variable that holds the memory address of another variable of a given data type (or an undefined type). So a pointer variable indirectly refers to a value. The definition of a pointer type is not based on a specific keyword, but uses a special character, the caret (^):

```
type
   TPointerToInt = ^Integer;
```

Once you have defined a pointer variable, you can assign to it the address of another variable of the same type, using the @ operator:

```
var
   P: ^Integer;
   X: Integer;

begin
   P := @X;
   // change the value in two different ways
   X := 10;
   P^ := 20;
```

When you have a pointer P, with the expression P you refer to the address of the memory location the pointer is referring to, and with the expression P^ you refer to the actual content of that memory location. For this reason in the code fragment above P^ corresponds to X.

Instead of referring to an existing memory location, a pointer can refer to a new memory block dynamically allocated (on the memory heap[26]) with the New procedure[27]. In this case, when you don't need the value accessed by the pointer anymore, you'll also have to get rid of the memory you've dynamically allocated, by calling the Dispose procedure.

If you don't dispose of the memory after using it, your program may eventually use up all the available memory and crash. This is known as a *Memory Leak*.

---

26 Memory management in general and the way the heap works in particular are covered in Chapter 8. In short, the heap is a (large) area of memory in which you can allocate and release blocks of memory in no given order.

27 As an alternative to New and Dispose you can use GetMem and FreeMem. According to the Delphi help, however, "*it is considered preferable to use the New and Dispose procedures*".

Here is a code snippet[28]:

```
var
   P: ^Integer;
begin
   // initialization
   New (P);
   // operations
   P^ := 20;
   writeln (P^);
   // termination
   Dispose (P);
end;
```

If a pointer has no value, you can assign the nil value to it. Then you can test whether a pointer is nil to see if it currently refers to a value.

This is often used, because dereferencing (that is accessing the value in the address stored in the pointer) an invalid pointer causes an access violation (also known as a general protection fault):

```
var
   P: ^Integer;
begin
   P := nil;
   writeln (P^);
```

You can see an example of the effect of this code by running the Pointers example after uncommenting the last few lines of code. The error you'll see should be similar to:

```
Exception EAccessViolation in module Pointers.exe at
000083AC. Access violation at address 004083AC in module
'Pointers.exe'. Read of address 00000000.
```

One of the ways to make pointer data access safer, is to add a "pointer is not null" safe-check like the following:

```
   if P <> nil then
      writeln (P^);
```

An alternative way, generally preferable for readability reasons, is to use the Assigned pseudo-function[29]:

---

28 This code should indeed use a try-finally block, a topic I decided not to introduce in this book, because despite its relevance it was not part of the traditional Pascal language or its Turbo Pascal extensions.

29 Assigned is not a real function, because it is "resolved" by the compiler producing the proper code.

```
if Assigned(P) then
  writeln (P^);
```

Delphi also defines a `Pointer` data type, which indicates untyped pointers (such as `void*` in the C language). If you use an untyped pointer you should use `GetMem` instead of `New`. The `GetMem` procedure is required each time the size of the memory variable to allocate is not defined.

The fact that pointers are seldom necessary in Pascal is an interesting advantage of this environment. Nonetheless, understanding pointers is important for advanced programming and for a full understanding of Delphi object model, which use pointers "behind the scenes."

File Types

Another Pascal-specific type constructor is the *file* type. File types represent physical disk files, certainly a peculiarity of the Pascal language. You can define a new file data type as follows[30]:

```
type
  IntFile = file of Integer;
```

Then you can open a physical file associated with this structure and write integer values to it or read the current values from the file.

The use of files in Pascal is quite straightforward, but in Delphi there are also some components that are capable of storing or loading their contents to or from a file. There is some serialization support, in the form of streams, and there is also database support.

Conclusion

This chapter discussing user-defined data types completes our coverage of the Pascal type system. Now we are ready to look into the statements the language provides to operate on the variables we've defined.

---

30 Files-based examples are covered in Chapter 12. Notice, however, that the file type is not available in Delphi for .NET.

Chapter 5: Statements

If the data types are one of the foundations of Pascal programming, the other are statements. In its time, this idea was clarified by Nicklaus Wirth's outstanding book "Algorithms + Data Structures = Programs", published by Prentice Hall in February 1976 (a classic book, still reprinted and available).

Statements of the programming language are based on keywords and other elements which allow you to indicate to a compiler a sequence of operations to perform. Statements are often enclosed in procedures or functions, as we'll see in the next chapter. Now we'll just focus on the basic types of commands you can use to create a program.

Simple and Compound Statements

A Pascal statement is simple when it doesn't contain any other statement. Examples of simple statements are assignment statements and procedure calls. Simple statements are separated by a semicolon:

```
X := Y + Z;   // assignment
Randomize;    // procedure call
```

Marco Cantù, Essential Pascal

Usually, statements are part of a compound statement, bracketed within the words begin and end. A compound statement can appear anywhere a simple Pascal statement can appear. Here is an example:

```
begin
  A := B;
  C := A * 2;
end;
```

The semicolon after the last statement of the compound statement (that is, before the end) isn't required, as in the following:

```
begin
  A := B;
  C := A * 2
end;
```

Both versions are correct. The first version has a useless (but harmless) semicolon. This semicolon is, in fact, a null statement or an empty statement; that is, a statement with no code[31].

Although these final semicolons serve no purpose, I tend to use them and suggest you do the same. Sometimes after you've written a couple of lines you might want to add one more statement. If the last semicolon is missing you have to remember to add it, so it is usually better to add it in the first place.

Assignment Statements

Assignments in Pascal use the colon-equal operator (:=), an odd notation for programmers who are used to other languages[32]. The = operator, which is used for assignments in many other languages, in Pascal is used to test for equality.

By using different symbols for an assignment and an equality test, the Pascal compiler (like the C compiler) can translate source code faster, because it

---

31 Notice that, at times, null statements can be specifically used inside loops or in other particular cases:

```
while condition_with_side_effect do
  ; // null or empty statement
```

32 Except people, like the book editor, whose first introduction was Algol and first professional language was PL/1...

doesn't need to examine the context in which the operator is used to determine its meaning. The use of different operators also makes the code easier for people to read. Truly Pascal picked two different operators than C (and syntactic derivatives like Java, C#, JavaScript), which uses = for assignment and == for equality test.

The two elements of an assignment are often called *rvalue* and *lvalue*, for right value (the variable or memory location you are assigning from) and left value, the value of the expressions being assigned.

The result of the expression is generally copied to the variable. When you copy a record or an array, for example, the entire data structure is copied to a new memory location, an operation that might be time-consuming. As we'll see in Chapter 7, strings are managed in a different way.

Conditional Statements

A conditional statement is used to execute either one of the statements it contains or none of them, depending on a specified test. There are two basic flavors of conditional statements: if statements and case statements.

If Statements

The if statement can be used to execute a statement only if a certain condition is met (if-then) or to choose between two different alternatives (if-then-else). The condition is described with a Boolean expression.

A simple Pascal example will demonstrate how to write conditional statements. In this program we'll ask the user for input, by using the read function with a single character as parameter:

```
var
  aChar: Char;

begin
  write ('Enter a character: ');
  readln (aChar);

  if aChar = 'a' then
    writeln ('You pressed [a]');
```

If you enter the *a* character (lowercase *A*), the program will show a simple message. Otherwise nothing happens. In a case like this, it would probably be better to make this more explicit, as with the following code snippet, which uses an if-then-else statement:

```
// if-then-else statement
if aChar = 'b' then
  writeln ('You pressed [b]')
else
  writeln ('You pressed something else than [b]');
```

Notice that you cannot have a semicolon after the first statement and before the else keyword or the compiler will issue a syntax error. The if-then-else statement is, in fact, a single statement, so you cannot place a semicolon in the middle of it.

An if statement can be quite complex. The condition can be turned into a series of conditions (using the and, or, and not Boolean operators), or the if statement can nest a second if statement. The last part of the IfTest example demonstrates these cases:

```
// statement with a double condition
// checks for a lowercase char
if (aChar >= 'a') and (aChar <= 'z') then
  writeln ('lowercase');

// compound if statement
if aChar >= Char(32) then
begin
  if (aChar >= '0') and (aChar <= '9') then
    writeln ('a number')
  else
    writeln ('not a number');
end
else
  writeln ('non-printable char');
```

Look at the code carefully and run the program to see if you understand everything (you can use the Tab key to enter a non printable character). When you have doubts about a programming construct, writing a very simple test program such as this can help you learn a lot. You can consider more options and Boolean expressions and increase the complexity of this small example, making any test you like.

Case Statements

If your if statements become very complex, at times you can replace them with case statements. A case statement consists of an expression used to select a value, a list of possible values, or a range of values. These values are constants, and they must be unique and of an ordinal type. Eventually, there can be an else statement that is executed if none of the labels correspond to the value of the selector. Here are two simple examples (part of the CaseTest project):

```pascal
case Number of
  1: Text := 'One';
  2: Text := 'Two';
  3: Text := 'Three';
end;

case aChar of
  '+' : Text := 'Plus sign';
  '-' : Text := 'Minus sign';
  '*', '/': Text := 'Multiplication or division';
  '0'..'9': Text := 'Number';
  'a'..'z': Text := 'Lowercase character';
  'A'..'Z': Text := 'Uppercase character';
else
  Text := 'Unknown character: ' + aChar;
end;
```

It is considered a good practice to include the else part to signal an undefined or unexpected condition.

Loops in Pascal

The Pascal language has the typical repetitive statements of most programming languages, including for, while, and repeat statements. Most of what these loops do will be familiar if you've used other programming languages, so I'll only cover them briefly.

The For Loop

The for loop in Pascal is strictly based on a counter, which can be either increased or decreased each time the loop is executed. Here is a simple example of a for loop used to add the first ten numbers.

```
var
   total, I: Integer;

begin
   total := 0;
   for I := 1 to 10 do
     total := total + I;
```

This same for statement could have been written using a reverse counter:

```
var
   total, I: Integer;

begin
   total := 0;
   for I := 10 downto 1 do
     total := total + I;
```

The for loop in Pascal is less flexible than in other languages (it is not possible to specify an increment different than one), but it is simple and easy to understand. If you want to test for a more complex condition, or to provide a customized counter, you need to use a while or repeat statement, instead of a for loop.

The counter of a for loop doesn't need to be a number. It can be a value of any ordinal type, such as a character or an enumerated type. Here is an example with characters:

```
var
   aChar: Char;

begin
   for aChar := 'a' to 'z' do
   begin
     write (aChar);
     write (' ');
   end;
```

Here is another example with an enumeration:

```
type
   TSuit = (Club, Diamond, Heart, Spade);
```

```
var
  aSuit: TSuit;

begin
  for aSuit := Club to Spade do
    ...
```

All these code fragments are part of the ForTest example. The last loop can also be written to explicitly operate on each element of the enumeration by writing:

```
for aSuit := Low (TSuit) to High (TSuit) do
```

Recent versions of Delphi introduce a new form of loop, called for-in, which resembles the traditional Visual Basic for-each loop. In this kind of for loop the cycle operates on each element of an array, a list, or some other form of container.[33]

While and Repeat Statements

The difference between the while-do loop and the repeat-until loop is that the code of the repeat statement is always executed at least once. You can easily understand why, by looking at a simple example:

```
while (I <= 100) and (J <= 100) do
begin
  // use I and J to compute something...
  I := I + 1;
  J := J + 1;
end;

repeat
  // use I and J to compute something...
  I := I + 1;
  J := J + 1;
until (I > 100) or (J > 100);
```

If the initial value of I or J is greater than 100, the statements inside the repeat-until loop are executed once anyway.

The other key difference between these two loops is that the repeat-until loop has a *reversed* condition. This loop is executed as long as the condition is *not* met. When the condition is met, the loop terminates. This is the opposite of a while-do loop, which is executed while the condition is true. For

---

33 The details of the for-in loop are covered in my "Delphi 2007 Handbook".

this reason I had to reverse the condition in the code above to obtain a similar effect.[34]

Examples of Loops

To explore the details of loops, let's look at a small Pascal example. The LoopsTest program highlights the difference between a loop with a fixed counter and a loop with an almost random counter. The first loop displays a number of strings:

```
var
  I: Integer;
begin
  for I := 1 to 20 do
    writeln ('String ' + IntToStr (I));
end;
```

The second fragment is slightly more complex. In this case, there is a while loop based on a counter, which is increased randomly. To accomplish this, I've called the Randomize procedure, which resets the random number generator, and the Random function with a range value of 100. The result of this function is a number between 0 and 99, chosen randomly. The series of random numbers control how many times the while loop is executed.

```
var
  I: Integer;
begin
  Randomize;
  I := 0;
  while I < 1000 do
  begin
    I := I + Random (100);
    writeln ('Random Number: ' + IntToStr (I));
  end;
end;
```

Each time you run the program, the numbers are different, because they depend on the random-number generator. The following is the output of two separate executions, in parallel:

```
Random Number: 25       Random Number: 82
Random Number: 68       Random Number: 130
Random Number: 131      Random Number: 140
```

---

34 This property is formally known as the "De Morgan's" laws (found herehttp://en.wikipedia.org/wiki/De_Morgan%27s_laws)

```
Random Number: 192          Random Number: 186
Random Number: 263          Random Number: 195
Random Number: 347          Random Number: 196
Random Number: 379          Random Number: 214
Random Number: 437          Random Number: 311
Random Number: 531          Random Number: 403
Random Number: 583          Random Number: 429
Random Number: 660          Random Number: 468
Random Number: 683          Random Number: 515
Random Number: 689          Random Number: 608
Random Number: 751          Random Number: 628
Random Number: 775          Random Number: 722
Random Number: 798          Random Number: 776
Random Number: 888          Random Number: 824
Random Number: 910          Random Number: 889
Random Number: 948          Random Number: 967
Random Number: 970          Random Number: 1062
Random Number: 1019
```

Notice that not only are the generated numbers different each time, but so is the number of items. This `while` loop is executed a random numbers of times. If you execute the program several times in a row, you'll see that the output has a different number of lines.

You can alter the standard flow of a loop's execution using the `Break` and `Continue` system procedures. The first interrupts the loop; the second is used to jump directly to the loop test or counter increment, continuing with the next iteration of the loop (unless the condition is zero or the counter has reached its highest value)[35]. Two more system procedures, `Exit` and `Halt`, let you immediately return from the current function or procedure or terminate the program.

The With Statement

The last kind of Pascal statement I'll focus on is the `with` statement, which used to be peculiar to this programming language (although it has since been introduced in JavaScript and Visual Basic) and can be very useful in Pascal programming.

---

35 I find it preferable to use standard conditional statements (`if`) rather than `Break` and `Continue`, as the code will generally be more clear.

The with statement is nothing but a shorthand. When you need to refer to a record type variable (or an object), instead of repeating its name every time, you can use a with statement. For example, while presenting the record type, I wrote this code:

```
type
  TMyDate = record
    Year: Integer;
    Month: Byte;
    Day: Byte;
  end;

var
  BirthDay: TMyDate;

begin
  BirthDay.Year := 2007;
  BirthDay.Month := 2;
  BirthDay.Day := 14;
```

Using a with statement, I can improve the final part of this code, as follows:

```
with BirthDay do
begin
  Year := 2008;
  Month := 2;
  Day := 14;
end;
```

This approach can be used in Pascal programs to refer to components and other class types. When you work with components or classes in general, the with statement allows you to skip writing some code, particularly for nested fields.

For example in Delphi VCL code, suppose that you need to change the Width and the Color of the drawing pen for a form. You can write the following code:

```
Form1.Canvas.Pen.Width := 2;
Form1.Canvas.Pen.Color := clRed;
```

But it is certainly easier to write this code:

```
with Form1.Canvas.Pen do
begin
  Width := 2;
  Color := clRed;
end;
```

When you are writing complex code, the with statement can be effective and spares you the declaration of some temporary variables, but it has a drawback. It can make the code less readable, particularly when you are working with different enums, records and objects that have similar or corresponding properties. A further drawback is that using the `with` statement can allow subtle logic errors in the code that the compiler will not detect. This example shows how a logic error can be correctly missed by the compiler when with is used in conjunction with derived objects:

```
with Button1 do
begin
  Width := 200;
  Caption := 'New Caption';
  Color := clRed;
end;
```

This code changes the `Caption` and the `Width` of the button, but it affects the `Color` property of the form, not that of the button! The reason is that the `TButton` components don't have the `Color` property, and since the code is executed for a form object (we are writing a method of the form) this object is accessed by default. If we had instead written:

```
Button1.Width := 200;
Button1.Caption := 'New Caption';
Button1.Color := clRed; // error!
```

the compiler would have issued an error. In general, we can say that since the `with` statement introduces new identifiers in the current scope, we might hide existing identifiers, or wrongfully access another identifier in the same scope (as in the first version of this code fragment). Even considering this kind of drawback, I suggest you get used to `with` statements, because they can be really very handy, and at times even make the code more readable. You should, however, avoid using multiple `with` statements, such as:

```
with ListBox1, Button1 do...
```

The code following this would probably be highly unreadable, because for each property defined in this block you would need to think about which component it refers to, depending on the respective properties and the order of the components in the `with` statement.

Speaking of readability, Pascal has no `endif` or `endcase` statement. If an `if` statement has a `begin-end` block, then the end of the block marks the end of the statement. The `case` statement, instead, is always terminated by an `end`. All these `end` statements, often found one after the other, can make the code difficult to follow. Only by tracing the indentations can you see which statement a particular `end` refers to. A common way to solve this problem

Marco Cantù, Essential Pascal

and make the code more readable is to add a comment after the end statement indicating its role, as in:

```
end; // if
```

Summary

This chapter has described how to code conditional statements and loops. Instead of writing long lists of such statements, programs are usually split into routines, procedures or functions. This is the topic of the next chapter, which also introduces some advanced elements.

Chapter 6: Procedures And Functions

Another important idea emphasized by Pascal is the concept of the routine, basically a series of statements with a unique name, which can be activated many times by using their name. This way you avoid having to write the same statements over and over, and will have a single version of the code used in many places through the program. From this point of view, you can think of routines as a basic code encapsulation mechanism. I'll get back to this topic with an example after I introduce the Pascal routines syntax.

Pascal Procedures and Functions

In Pascal, a routine can assume two forms: a procedure and a function. In theory, a procedure is an operation you ask the computer to perform, a function is a computation returning a value. This difference is emphasized by the fact that a function has a result, a return value, while a procedure doesn't. Both types of routines can have multiple parameters of specified data types.

In practice, however, the difference between functions and procedures is very limited: you can call a function to perform some work and then skip the result (which might be an optional error code or something like that) or you can call a procedure which passes back a result within its parameters (more on reference parameters later in this chapter).

Here are the definitions of a procedure and two versions of the same function, using a slightly different syntax:

```
procedure Hello;
begin
  writeln ('Hello world!');
end;

function Double (Value: Integer) : Integer;
begin
  Double := Value * 2;
end;

// or, as an alternative
function Double2 (Value: Integer) : Integer;
begin
  Result := Value * 2;
end;
```

The use of Result instead of the function name to assign the return value of a function is becoming quite popular, and tends to make the code more readable. Once these routines have been defined, you can call them one or more times. You call the procedure to make it perform its task, and call a function to compute the value:

```
// call the procedure
Hello;

// call the function
X := Double (100);
Y := Double (X);
writeln (IntToStr (Y));
```

This is the encapsulation code concept I've introduced before in practice. When you call the *Double* function, you don't need to know the algorithm used to implement it. If you later find out a better way to double numbers, you can easily change the code of the function, but the calling code will remain unchanged (although executing it will be faster!). The same principle can be applied to the *Hello* procedure: We can modify the program output by changing the code of this procedure, and the main program code will automatically change its effect. Here is how we can change the code:

```
procedure Hello;
begin
  writeln ('Hello world, again!');
end;
```

When you call an existing Pascal function or procedure you need to remember the number and type of the parameters[36].

Reference Parameters

Pascal routines allow parameter passing by value and by reference. Passing parameters by value is the default: the value is copied on the stack and the routine uses and manipulates the copy, not the original value.

Passing a parameter by reference means that its value is not copied onto the stack in the formal parameter of the routine (avoiding a copy often means that the program executes faster). Instead, the program refers to the original value, also in the code of the routine. This allows the procedure or function to change the value of the parameter. Parameter passing by reference is expressed by the *var* keyword.

This technique is available in most programming languages. It isn't present in C, but has been introduced in C++, where you use the & (pass by reference) symbol. In Visual Basic every parameter not specified as ByVal is passed by reference. Here is an example of passing a parameter by reference using the var keyword:

```
procedure DoubleTheValue (var Value: Integer);
begin
  Value := Value * 2;
end;
```

In this case, the parameter is used both to pass a value to the procedure and to return a new value to the calling code. When you write:

```
var
  X: Integer;
```

---

36 Delphi editor helps you by suggesting the parameters list of a function or procedure with a fly-by hint as soon as you type its name and the open parenthesis. This feature is called Code Parameters and is part of the Code Insight technology.

```
begin
  X := 10;
  DoubleTheValue (X);
```

the value of the X variable becomes 20, because the function uses a reference to the original memory location of X, affecting its initial value.

Passing parameters by reference makes sense for ordinal types, for old-fashioned strings, and for large records[37]. Delphi strings have a slightly different behavior: they behave as references, but if you change one of the string variables referring to the same string in memory, this is copied before updating it. A long string passed as a value parameter behaves as a reference only in terms of memory usage and speed of the operation. But if you modify the value of the string, the original value is not affected. On the contrary, if you pass the long string by reference, you can alter the original value.

Delphi 3 introduced a new kind of parameter, out. An out parameter has no initial value and is used only to return a value. These parameters should be used only for COM procedures and functions; in general, it is better to stick with the more efficient var parameters. Except for not having an initial value, out parameters behave like var parameters.

Constant Parameters

As an alternative to reference parameters, you can use a const parameter. Since you cannot assign a new value to a constant parameter inside the routine, the compiler can optimize parameter passing. The compiler can choose an approach similar to reference parameters (or a const reference in C++ terms), but the behavior will remain similar to value parameters, because the original value won't be affected by the routine.

In fact, if you try to compile the following (silly) code, Delphi will issue an error:

```
function DoubleTheValue (const Value: Integer): Integer;
begin
  Value := Value * 2;        // compiler error
```

---

37 Pascal objects, in fact, are invariably passed by value, because they are references themselves. For this reason passing an object by reference makes little sense (apart from very special cases), because it corresponds to passing a "reference to a reference."

```
   Result := Value;
end;
```

Open Array Parameters

Unlike C, a Pascal function or procedure always has a fixed number of parameters. However, there is a way to pass a varying number of parameters to a routine using an open array. The basic definition of an open array parameter is that of a typed open array. This means you indicate the type of the parameter but do not know how many elements of that type the array is going to have. Here is an example of such a definition:

```
function Sum (const A: array of Integer): Integer;
var
  I: Integer;
begin
  Result := 0;
  for I := Low(A) to High(A) do
    Result := Result + A[I];
end;
```

Using High(A) we can get the upper bound of the array. Notice also the use of the return value of the function, Result, to store temporary values. You can call this function by passing to it an *array-of-Integer* expression:

```
X := Sum ([10, Y, 27*I]);
```

Given an array of Integer, of any size, you can pass it directly to a routine requiring an open array parameter or, instead, you can call the slice function to pass only a portion of the array (as indicated by its second parameter). Here is an example, where the complete array is passed as parameter:

```
var
  List: array [1..10] of Integer;
  X, I: Integer;
begin
  // initialize the array
  for I := Low (List) to High (List) do
    List [I] := I * 2;
  // call
  X := Sum (List);
```

If you want to pass only a portion of the array to the Sum function, simply call it this way using the standard Slice function:

```
X := Sum (Slice (List, 5));
```

Did you notice how the parameter to one function can be the result of another? You can find all the code fragments presented in this section in the OpenArr example.

Typed open arrays are fully compatible with dynamic arrays (introduced in Delphi 4 and covered in Chapter 8). Dynamic arrays use the same syntax as open arrays, with the difference that you can use a notation such as array of Integer to declare a variable, not just to pass a parameter.

Type-Variant Open Array Parameters

Besides these typed open arrays, Delphi allows you to define type-variant or untyped open arrays. This special kind of array has an undefined number of values, which can be handy for passing parameters.

Technically, the construct array of const allows you to pass an array with an undefined number of elements of different types to a routine at once. For example, here is the definition of the Format function (we'll see how to use this function in Chapter 7, covering strings):

```
function Format (const Format: string;
  const Args: array of const): string;
```

The second parameter is an open array, which gets an undefined number of values. In fact, you can call this function in the following ways:

```
N := 20;
S := 'Total:';
writeln (Format ('Total: %d', [N]));
writeln (Format ('Int: %d, Float: %f', [N, 12.4]));
writeln (Format ('%s %d', [S, N * 2]));
```

Notice that you can pass a parameter as either a constant value, the value of a variable, or an expression. Declaring a function of this kind is simple, but how do you code it? How do you know the types of the parameters? The values of a type-variant open array parameter are compatible with the TVarRec type elements[38].

The TVarRec record has the following structure:

```
type
  TVarRec = record
    case Byte of
      vtInteger:     (VInteger: Integer; VType: Byte);
      vtBoolean:     (VBoolean: Boolean);
      vtChar:        (VChar: Char);
      vtExtended:    (VExtended: PExtended);
      vtString:      (VString: PShortString);
      vtPointer:     (VPointer: Pointer);
      vtPChar:       (VPChar: PChar);
      vtObject:      (VObject: TObject);
      vtClass:       (VClass: TClass);
      vtWideChar:    (VWideChar: WideChar);
      vtPWideChar:   (VPWideChar: PWideChar);
      vtAnsiString:  (VAnsiString: Pointer);
      vtCurrency:    (VCurrency: PCurrency);
      vtVariant:     (VVariant: PVariant);
      vtInterface:   (VInterface: Pointer);
  end;
```

Each possible record has the VType field, although this is not easy to see at first because it is declared only once, along with the actual Integer-size data (generally a reference or a pointer). Using this information we can actually write a function capable of operating on different data types. In the SumAll function example, I want to be able to sum values of different types, transforming strings to integers, characters to the corresponding ordinal value, and adding 1 for True Boolean values.

The code is based on a case statement, and is quite simple, although we have to dereference pointers quite often:

```
function SumAll (const Args: array of const): Extended;
var
  I: Integer;
begin
  Result := 0;
  for I := Low(Args) to High (Args) do
    case Args [I].VType of
      vtInteger: Result :=
```

---

38 Do not confuse the TVarRec record with the TVarData record used by the Variant type itself. These two structures have a different aim and are not compatible. Even the list of possible types is different, because TVarRec can hold Delphi data types, while TVarData can hold Windows OLE data types.

```
          Result + Args [I].VInteger;
        vtBoolean:
          if Args [I].VBoolean then
            Result := Result + 1;
        vtChar:
          Result := Result + Ord (Args [I].VChar);
        vtExtended:
          Result := Result + Args [I].VExtended^;
        vtString, vtAnsiString:
          Result := Result + StrToIntDef ((
            Args [I].VString^), 0);
        vtWideChar:
          Result := Result + Ord (Args [I].VWideChar);
        vtCurrency:
          Result := Result + Args [I].VCurrency^;
    end; // case
end;
```

I've added this code to the OpenArr example, which calls the SumAll function with the following code:

```
var
  X: Extended;
  Y: Integer;
begin
  Y := 10;
  X := SumAll ([Y * Y, 'k', True, 10.34, '99999']);
  writeln (Format (
    'SumAll ([Y*Y, ''k'', True, 10.34, ''99999'']) => %n',
    [X]));
end;
```

You can see the output of this call below:

```
SumAll ([Y*Y, 'k', True, 10.34, '99999']) => 10,217.34
```

Delphi Calling Conventions

The 32-bit version of Delphi introduced a new approach to passing parameters, known as *fastcall*: Whenever possible, up to three parameters can be passed in CPU registers, making the function call much faster. The fast calling convention (used by default since Delphi 3) is indicated by the register keyword.

The problem is that this is the default convention, and functions using it are not compatible with Windows: the functions of the Win32 API must be declared using the `stdcall` calling convention, a mixture of the original `pascal` calling convention of the Win16 API and the `cdecl` calling convention of the C language.

There is generally no reason not to use the new fast calling convention, unless you are making external Windows calls or defining Windows callback functions. We'll see an example using the `stdcall` convention before the end of this chapter. You can find a summary of Delphi calling conventions in the Calling conventions topic under Delphi help.

What Is a Method?

If you have already worked with Delphi or read the manuals, you have probably heard about the term "method". A method is a special kind of function or procedure that is related to a data type, a class. In Delphi, every time we handle an event, we need to define a method, generally a procedure. In general, however, the term method is used to indicate both functions and procedures related to a class.

Here is an empty method automatically added by Delphi to the source code of a form:

```
procedure TForm1.Button1Click(Sender: TObject);
begin
  {here goes your code}
end;
```

Forward Declarations

When you need to use an identifier (of any kind), the compiler must have already seen some sort of declaration to know what the identifier refers to. For this reason, you usually provide a full declaration before using any routine. However, there are cases in which this is not possible. If procedure A calls procedure B, and procedure B calls procedure A, when you start writing the code, you will need to call a routine for which the compiler still hasn't seen a declaration.

If you want to declare the existence of a procedure or function with a certain name and given parameters, without providing its actual code, you can write the procedure or function followed by the forward keyword:

```
procedure Hello; forward;
```

Later on, the code should provide a full definition of the procedure, but this can be called even before it is fully defined. Here is a silly example, just to give you the idea:

```
procedure DoubleHello; forward;

procedure Hello;
begin
  if MessageDlg ('Do you want a double message?',
      mtConfirmation, [mbYes, mbNo], 0) = mrYes then
    DoubleHello
  else
    ShowMessage ('Hello');
end;

procedure DoubleHello;
begin
  Hello;
  Hello;
end;
```

This approach allows you to write mutual recursion: DoubleHello calls Hello, but Hello might call DoubleHello, too. Of course there must be a condition to terminate the recursion, to avoid a stack overflow. You can find this code, with some slight changes, in the DoubleH example.

Although a forward procedure declaration is not very common in Pascal, there is a similar case that is much more frequent. When you declare a procedure or function in the interface portion of a unit (more on units in the next chapter), it is considered a forward declaration, even if the forward keyword is not present. Actually you cannot write the body of a routine in the interface portion of a unit. At the same time, you must provide in the same unit the actual implementation of each routine you have declared[39].

---

39 The same holds for the declaration of a method inside a class type that was automatically generated by the Delphi IDE (as you added an event to a form or its components). The event handlers declared inside a TForm class are forward declarations: the code will be provided in the implementation portion of the unit.

Marco Cantù, Essential Pascal

Procedural Types

Another unique feature of Object Pascal is the presence of procedural types. These are really an advanced language topic, which only a few Delphi programmers will use regularly. However, since we will discuss related topics in later chapters (specifically, method pointers, a technique heavily used by Delphi), it's worth a quick look at them here. If you are a novice programmer, you can skip this section for now, and come back to it when you feel ready.

In Pascal, there is the concept of procedural type (which is similar to the C language concept of function pointer). The declaration of a procedural type indicates the list of parameters and, in the case of a function, the return type. For example, you can declare a new procedural type, with an Integer parameter passed by reference, with this code:

```
type
  TIntProc = procedure (var Num: Integer);
```

This procedural type is compatible with any routine having exactly the same parameters (or the same function signature, to use C jargon). Here is an example of a compatible routine[40]:

```
procedure DoubleTheValue (var Value: Integer);
begin
  Value := Value * 2;
end;
```

Procedural types can be used for two different purposes: you can declare variables of a procedural type or pass a procedural type (that is, a function pointer) as parameter to another routine. Given the preceding type and procedure declarations, you can write this code:

```
var
  IP: TIntProc;
  X: Integer;
begin
  IP := DoubleTheValue;
  X := 5;
  IP (X);
end;
```

This code has the same effect as the following shorter version:

---

40 In the 16-bit version of Delphi, routines must be declared using the far directive in order to be used as actual values of a procedural type.

```
var
  X: Integer;
begin
  X := 5;
  DoubleTheValue (X);
end;
```

The first version is clearly more complex, so why should we use it? In some cases, being able to decide which function to call and actually calling it later on can be useful. It is possible to build a complex example showing this approach. However, I prefer to let you explore a fairly simple one, named ProcType. This example is more complex than those we have seen so far to make the situation a little more realistic.

This example is based on two procedures. One procedure is used to double the value of the parameter. This procedure is similar to the version I've already shown in this section. A second procedure is used to triple the value of the parameter, and therefore is named TripleTheValue:

```
procedure TripleTheValue (var Value: Integer);
begin
  Value := Value * 3;
  writeln ('Value tripled: ' + IntToStr (Value));
end;
```

Both procedures display what is going on, to let us know that they have been called. This is a simple debugging feature you can use to test whether or when a certain portion of code is executed, instead of using a breakpoint.

Instead of calling this functions directly, to demonstrate the use of procedural types, I've instead used a longer but more interesting approach. Each time a user enters 2 or 3 on the keyboard, one of the procedures is stored in a variable:

```
var
  ch: Char;
  IP: TIntProc;
  X: Integer;

begin
  // initial defaults
  X := 10;
  IP := DoubleTheValue;

  while True do
  begin
    // read and call
    read (ch);
```

```
    case ch of
      '2': IP := DoubleTheValue;
      '3': IP := TripleTheValue;
      'x': Break;
    else
      IP (X);
  end;
end;
```

When the user presses any other key (the `else` branch of the `case` above), the procedure we have stored is executed. You can see a more practical example of the use of procedural types in Chapter 9, in the section *A Windows Callback Function*.

Function Overloading

The idea of overloading is simple: The compiler allows you to define two functions or procedures using the same name, provided that the parameters are different. By checking the parameters, in fact, the compiler can determine which of the versions of the routine you want to call. Consider this series of functions extracted from the Math unit of the VCL:

```
function Min (A,B: Integer): Integer; overload;
function Min (A,B: Int64): Int64; overload;
function Min (A,B: Single): Single; overload;
function Min (A,B: Double): Double; overload;
function Min (A,B: Extended): Extended; overload;
```

When you call `Min (10, 20)`, the compiler easily determines that you're calling the first function of the group, so the return value will be an Integer.

The basic rules are two:

- Each version of the routine must be followed by the `overload` keyword.

- The differences must be in the number or type of the parameters, or both. The return type cannot be used to distinguish among two routines.

Here are three overloaded versions of a `ShowMsg` procedure I've added to the OverDef example (an application demonstrating overloading and default parameters):

```
procedure ShowMsg (str: string); overload;
begin
  writeln ('Message: ' + str);
end;

procedure ShowMsg (FormatStr: string;
  Params: array of const); overload;
begin
  writeln ('Message: ' + Format (FormatStr, Params));
end;

procedure ShowMsg (I: Integer; Str: string); overload;
begin
  ShowMsg (IntToStr (I) + ' ' + Str);
end;
```

The three functions show a message box with a string, after optionally formatting the string in different ways. Here are the three calls[41] of the program:

```
ShowMsg ('Hello');
ShowMsg ('Total = %d.', [100]);
ShowMsg (10, 'MBytes');
```

And this is their effect:

```
Message: Hello
Message: Total = 100.
Message: 10 MBytes
```

The fact that each version of an overloaded routine must be properly marked implies that you cannot overload an existing routine of the same unit that is not marked with the overload keyword. (The error message you get when you try is:

```
Previous declaration of '<name>' was not marked with the
'overload' directive.
```

However, you can overload a routine that was originally declared in a different unit[42]. This is for compatibility with previous versions of Delphi, which allowed different units to reuse the same routine name. Notice anyway, that this special case is not really an extra feature of overloading as it seems to have little effect.

---

41 Delphi IDE's Code Parameters technology works very nicely with overloaded procedures and functions. As you type the open parenthesis after the routine name, all the available alternatives are listed. As you enter the parameters, Delphi uses their type to determine which of the alternatives are still available.

42 For more information on units see Chapter 11.

Marco Cantù, Essential Pascal

For example, you can add to a program (in this case the OverDef example) the following code:

```
procedure MessageBox (str: string); overload;
begin
  Windows.MessageBox (0, PChar(str), 'Title', MB_OK);
end;
```

This code doesn't overload the original MessageBox routine of the Windows API at all. In fact if you try to call the original version with:

```
MessageBox (0, 'Message', 'Title', MB_OK);
```

you'll get a nice error message indicating that some of the parameters are missing. The only way to call the official version instead of the local one is to refer explicitly to the unit, something that defeats the idea of overloading:

```
Windows.MessageBox (0, 'Message', 'Title', MB_OK);
```

Default Parameters

Another feature related to overloading, is that you can give a default value to the parameter or parameters of a function, so that you can call the function with or without the parameter. If the parameter is missing in the call, it will take the default value.

Let me show an example. We can define the following encapsulation of the write call, providing two default parameters:

```
procedure NewMessage (Msg: string;
  Caption: string = 'Message';
  Separator: string = sLineBreak);
begin
  write (Caption);
  write (': ');
  write (Msg);
  write (Separator);
end;
```

With this definition, we can call the procedure in each of the following ways:

```
NewMessage ('Something wrong here!');
NewMessage ('Something wrong here!', 'Attention');
NewMessage ('Hello', 'Message', '--');
```

This is the output:

```
Message: Something wrong here!
Attention: Something wrong here!
Message: Hello--
```

Notice that Delphi doesn't generate any special code to support default parameters; nor does it create multiple copies of the routines. The missing parameters are simply added by the compiler to the calling code. There is one important restriction affecting the use of default parameters: You cannot "skip" parameters. For example, you can't pass the third parameter to the function after omitting the second one.

This is the main rule for default parameters: In a call, you can only omit parameters starting from the last one. In other words, if you omit a parameter you must also omit the following ones.

There are a few other rules for default parameters as well:

- Parameters with default values must be at the end of the parameters list.

- Default values must be constants. Obviously, this limits the types you can use with default parameters. For example, a dynamic array or an interface type cannot have a default parameter other than `nil`; records cannot be used at all.

- Default parameters must be passed by value or as `const`. A reference (`var`) parameter cannot have a default value.

Using default parameters and overloading at the same time can cause quite a few problems, as the two features might conflict. For example, if I add to the previous example the following new version of the `NewMessage` procedure:

```
procedure NewMessage (Str: string; I: Integer = 0);
  overload;
begin
  writeln (Str + ': ' + IntToStr (I))
end;
```

then the compiler won't complain, as this is a legal definition. However, the call:

```
NewMessage ('Hello');
```

is flagged by the compiler as:

```
NewMessageTest.dpr(24):
E2251 Ambiguous overloaded call to 'NewMessage'
```

Notice that this error shows up in a line of code that compiled correctly before the new overloaded definition. In practice, we have no way to call the NewMessage procedure with one string parameter, as the compiler doesn't know whether we want to call the version with only the string parameter or the one with the string parameter and the integer parameter with a default value. When it has a similar doubt, the compiler stops and asks the programmer to state his or her intentions more clearly.

Summary

Writing procedure and functions is a key element of programming, and even methods (their OOP counterpart) share most of the features with them. Instead of moving on to object-oriented features, however, the next few chapters give you some details on other Pascal programming elements, starting with strings.

Chapter 7: Handling Strings

String handling in Pascal looks fairly simple, but behind the scenes the situation is quite complex. Pascal has a traditional way of handling strings, Windows has its own way, borrowed from the C language, and modern versions of Pascal include a powerful long string data type, which is now the default string type in Delphi.

Types of Strings

In the early days of Borland's Turbo Pascal and in 16-bit Delphi, the typical string type was a sequence of characters with a length byte at the beginning, indicating the current size of the string. Because the length is expressed by a single byte, it cannot exceed 255 characters, a very low value that creates many problems for string manipulation. Each string is defined with a fixed size (which by default is the maximum, 255), although you can declare shorter strings to save memory space.

Marco Cantù, Essential Pascal

A string type is similar to an array type. In fact, a string is almost an array of characters. This is demonstrated by the fact that you can access a specific string character using the [] notation, similar to the C language.

To overcome the limits of traditional Pascal strings, modern versions of Pascal support long strings. There are actually three string types:

- The ShortString type corresponds to the original Pascal strings, as described before. These strings have a limit of 255 characters and correspond to the strings in the 16-bit version of Delphi. Each element of a short string is of type ANSIChar (the standard character type).

- The ANSIString type corresponds to the new variable-length long strings. These strings are allocated dynamically, are reference counted (which means that you don't need to worry about releasing the memory that they use), and use a copy-on-write technique. The size of these strings is almost unlimited (they can store up to two billion characters!). They are also based on the ANSIChar type.

- The WideString type is similar to the ANSIString type but is based on the WideChar type (it stores Unicode characters). It is not as powerful and efficient as the standard string types, as its support for reference counting is not as complete.

Traditional Pascal Strings

Traditional Pascal strings are a very simple and effective data structure. You can declare a string holding a maximum of 20 characters by declaring:

```
var
  strShortName: ShortString [20];[43]
begin
  strShortName := 'marco';
```

The data will be allocated locally (on the stack, the memory area used by procedures and functions for their local variables) and not dynamically[44]. In

---

43 You can write this also with the classic notation, strShortName: string [20];

44 The string location holds the data itself, and not a pointer to the actual data as for long strings.

this specific case you'll end up using 21 bytes, 20 for the characters and one for the length. This is traditionally called the "length byte" and is stored at the beginning of the string data. Notice, in fact, that the string has a maximum size of 20 characters, but during its lifetime the length of the string it stores might vary. Given the assignment above, the actual length will be five and it will consume 6 bytes.

By declaring their dimension upfront, you are limited to a specific maximum size and cannot exceed it for any reason. Moreover, the maximum size you can declare is 255, simply because the length byte is a byte, so it can only represent a number ranging from 0 to 255.

On the other hand, short strings are very fast (as there is no dynamic allocation, cleanup, and no reference counting involved). With a fixed size, they can easily be stored in records and other data structures. Indeed, a fixed string size is a limitation, but one that a database developer, for example, will easily live with.

Short strings are not heavily used in Pascal these days, although they are certainly a key data structure of traditional Pascal. That's why in this chapter I prefer to focus on long strings.

Using Long Strings

If you simply use the string data type, you get either short strings or ANSI strings, depending on the value of the $H compiler directive. $H+ (the default) stands for long strings (the ANSIString type), which is what is used by the components of the Delphi library.

Pascal long strings are based on a reference-counting mechanism, which keeps track of how many string variables are referring to the same string in memory. This reference-counting is used also to free the memory when a string isn't used anymore-that is, when the reference count reaches zero.

If you want to increase the size of a string in memory but there is something else in the adjacent memory, then the string cannot grow in the same memory location, and a full copy of the string must therefore be made in another location. When this situation occurs, run-time support reallocates the string for you in a completely transparent way. You simply set the maximum size of the string with the `SetLength` procedure, effectively allocating the required amount of memory:

```
SetLength (String1, 200);
```

The `SetLength` procedure performs a memory request, not an actual memory allocation. It reserves the required memory space for future use, without actually using the memory. This technique is based on a feature of the Windows operating systems and is used by Delphi for all dynamic memory allocations. For example, when you request a very large array, its memory is reserved but not allocated.

Setting the length of a string is seldom necessary. The only case in which you must allocate memory for the long string using `SetLength` is when you have to pass the string as a parameter to a Windows API function (after the proper typecast), as I'll show you shortly.

Looking at Strings in Memory

To help you better understand the details of memory management for strings, I've written the simple StrRef example. In this program I declare two global strings: `Str1` and `Str2`. The program assigns a constant string to the first of the two variables and then assigns the second variable to the first:

```
Str1 := 'Hello';
Str2 := Str1;
```

Besides working on the strings, the program shows their internal status in a list box, using the following `StringStatus` function:

```
function StringStatus (const Str: string): string;
begin
  Result := 'Address: ' +
    IntToStr (Integer (Str)) +
    ', Length: ' +
    IntToStr (Length (Str)) +
    ', References: ' +
    IntToStr (PInteger (Integer (Str) - 8)^) +
    ', Value: ' + Str;
end;
```

It is vital in the `StringStatus` function to pass the string parameter as a `const` parameter. Passing this parameter by copying will cause the side effect of having one extra reference to the string while the function is being executed. By contrast, passing the parameter via a reference (var) or constant (const) parameter doesn't imply a further reference to the string. In this case I've used a const parameter, as the function is not supposed to modify the string.

To obtain the memory address of the string (useful to determine its actual identity and to see when two different strings refer to the same memory area), I've simply made a hard-coded typecast from the string type to the Integer type. Long strings are references-in practice, they're pointers: Their value holds the actual memory location of the string not the string itself.

To extract the reference count, I've based the code on the little-known fact that the length and reference count are actually stored in the string, before the actual text and before the position the string variable points to. The (negative) offset is -4 for the length of the string (a value you can extract more easily using the Length function) and -8 for the reference count[45].

By running this example, you should get two strings with the same content, the same memory location, and a reference count of 2:

```
Str1 - Address: 13419088, Length: 5,
   References: 2, Value: Hello
Str2 - Address: 13419088, Length: 5,
   References: 2, Value: Hello
```

Now if you change the value of one of the two strings (it doesn't matter which one), the memory location of the updated string will change. This is the effect of the copy-on-write technique. We can actually produce this effect by writing the following code:

```
Str1 [2] := 'a';
writeln ('Str1 [2] := ''a''');
writeln ('Str1 - ' + StringStatus (Str1));
writeln ('Str2 - ' + StringStatus (Str2));
```

This is the corresponding output:

```
Str1 - Address: 13419112, Length: 5,
   References: 1, Value: Hallo
Str2 - Address: 13419088, Length: 5,
   References: 1, Value: Hello
```

You can freely extend this example and use the *StringStatus* function to explore the behavior of long strings in many other circumstances.

---

45 Keep in mind that this internal information about offsets might change in any future version of Delphi; there is also no guarantee that similar undocumented features will be maintained in the future.

Delphi Strings and Windows PChars

Another important point in favor of using long strings is that they are null-terminated. This means that they are fully compatible with the C language null-terminated strings used by Windows. A null-terminated string is a sequence of characters followed by a byte that is set to zero (or null). This can be expressed in Delphi using a zero-based array of characters, the data type typically used to implement strings in the C language. This is the reason null-terminated character arrays are so common in the Windows API functions (which are based on the C language). Since Pascal's long strings are fully compatible with C null-terminated strings, you can simply use long strings and cast them to PChar when you need to pass a string to a Windows API function[46].

For example, to copy the name of the current Windows user into a PChar string (using the API function GetUserName) and then display it:

```
var
  Str1: string;
  nSize : Cardinal = 20;

begin
  SetLength (Str1, nSize);
  GetUserName(PChar (Str1), nSize);
  writeln (str1);
end;
```

You can find this code in the StringAndPChar example. Note that if you write this code without first allocating memory for the string with SetLength, the program will probably crash. If you are using a PChar to pass a value (and not to receive one, as in the code above), the code is simpler, because there is no need to define a temporary string and initialize it.

Having presented the nice picture, now I want to focus on the pitfalls. There are some problems that might arise when you convert a long string into a PChar. Essentially, the underlying problem is that after this conversion, you become responsible for the string and its contents, and Pascal won't help you

---

46 When you need to cast a WideString to a Windows-compatible type, you have to use PWideChar instead of PChar for the conversion. Wide strings are often used for COM programs.

any more. Consider the following small change in the StringAndPChar example, with some text added to the output string:

```
GetUserName(PChar (Str1), nSize);
writeln (str1 + '*');
```

This program compiles, but when you run it, you are in for a surprise: the output string will be:

```
Marco                    *
```

(This is my name, followed by 15 spaces, and followed by the *). The problem is that when Windows writes to the string (within the GetUserName API call), it doesn't set the length of the long Pascal string properly. Pascal can still use this string for output and can figure out when it ends by looking for the C-language null terminator (added by Windows), but it will append further text at the very and and (in other examples) skip any text you add after the null terminator.

How can we fix this problem? The solution is to tell the system to convert the string returned by the GetUserName API call back to a Pascal string. However, if you write the following code:

```
Str1 := String (Str1);
```

the system will ignore it, because converting a data type back into itself is a useless operation. To obtain the proper long Pascal string, you need to recast the string to a PChar and let Pascal convert it back again properly to a string:

```
Str1 := String (PChar (Str1));
```

Actually, you can skip the string conversion, because PChar-to-string conversions are automatic in Pascal, so you can write:

```
GetUserName(PChar (Str1), nSize);
Str1 := PChar (Str1);
writeln (Str1 + '*');
```

and obtain the expected output:

```
Marco*
```

An alternative is to reset the length of the Pascal string, using the length of the PChar string, by writing:

```
SetLength (Str1, StrLen (PChar (Str1)));
```

You can find most of this code snippets in the StringAndPChar example.

Formatting Strings

Using the plus (+) operator and some of the conversion functions (such as IntToStr) you can indeed build complex strings out of existing values. However, there is a different approach to formatting numbers, currency values, and other strings into a final string. You can use the powerful Format function or one of its companion functions.

The Format function requires as parameters a string with the basic text and some placeholders (usually marked by the % symbol) and an array of values, one for each placeholder. For example, to format two numbers into a string you can write:

```
Format ('First %d, Second %d', [n1, n2]);
```

where n1 and n2 are two Integer values. The first placeholder is replaced by the first value, the second matches the second, and so on. If the output type of the placeholder (indicated by the letter after the % symbol) doesn't match the type of the corresponding parameter, a runtime error occurs. Having no compile-time type checking is actually the biggest drawback of using the Format function. Similarly, not passing enough parameters causes a runtime error.

The Format function uses an open-array parameter (a parameter that can have an arbitrary number of values, as covered in Chapter 6). Besides using %d, you can use one of many other placeholders defined by this function and briefly listed the following table. These placeholders provide a default output for the given data type. However, you can use further format specifiers to alter the default output. A width specifier, for example, determines a fixed number of characters in the output, while a precision specifier indicates the number of decimal digits. For example,

```
Format ('%8d', [n1]);
```

converts the number n1 into an eight-character string, right-aligning the text (use the minus (-) symbol to specify left-justification) filling it with white spaces. Here is the list of formatting placeholders:

d (decimal)	The corresponding integer value is converted to a string of decimal digits.
x (hexadecimal)	The corresponding integer value is converted to a string of hexadecimal digits.

p (pointer)	The corresponding pointer value is converted to a string expressed with hexadecimal digits.
s (string)	The corresponding string, character, or PChar value is copied to the output string.
e (exponential)	The corresponding floating-point value is converted to a string based on scientific notation.
f (floating point)	The corresponding floating-point value is converted to a string based on floating point notation.
g (general)	The corresponding floating-point value is converted to the shortest possible decimal string using either floating-point or exponential notation.
n (number)	The corresponding floating-point value is converted to a floating-point string but also uses thousands separators.
m (money)	The corresponding floating-point value is converted to a string representing a currency amount. The conversion is based on regional settings-see the Delphi Help file under Currency and date/time formatting variables.

The best way to see examples of these conversions is to experiment with format strings yourself. To make this easier I've written the FmtTest program, which allows a user to provide formatting strings for integer and floating-point numbers. This program has much more interaction than most programs in this book. It first asks whether to perform either Integer of Floating number formatting, calling one of two specific routines depending on the input. This is the main portion of the program:

```
begin
  Done := False;
  while not Done do
  begin
    writeln ('Work with [I]nteger or [F]loating' +
      ' point numbers? [I or F or X to exit]');
    readln (chInput);

    case Upcase (chInput) of
      'I': TestFormatInteger;
      'F': TestFormatFloat;
      'X': Done := True;
    else
```

```
      writeln ('Wrong selection');
    end;
  end;
  writeln ('Bye');
  readln;
end.
```

Each of the routines asks for a numeric input and a format string, providing some suggestions:

```
procedure TestFormatInteger;
var
  n: Integer;
  strFmt: string;
begin
  writeln ('Enter value');
  readln (n);

  writeln ('Enter a format string: (examples below)');
  // suggestions omitted
  readln (strFmt);

  writeln (Format ('%d %s => %s',
    [n, strFmt, Format (strFmt, [n])]));
end;
```

The code basically does the formatting operation using the second input as format string and the value of the first input request for the value. The floating point number formatting is similar.

Summary

Strings are certainly a very common data type. Although you can safely use them in most cases without understanding how they work, this chapter should have made the exact behavior of strings clear, making it possible for you to use all the power of this data type.

Strings are handled in memory in a special dynamic way, as happens with dynamic arrays. This is the topic of the next chapter.

Chapter 8: Memory

This chapter covers memory handling, the various memory areas you can use in an application, and introduces dynamic arrays.

Global Memory

The global memory is the memory area for global variables. As you declare a global Integer variable, for example, the compiler will reserve 4 bytes of global memory for it. Regardless of the visibility of this global data (see Chapter 11 for units and their related visibility restrictions), it allocates global memory.

Global variables are allocated when the program starts in a specific global data memory, whose size and layout are defined by the compiler and linker. Global variables remain in that global memory area until the program terminates, even if they are used for a much more limited amount of time. This is why global memory usage is generally very limited in Pascal and Delphi applications, favoring the two dynamic memory areas applications can use, the heap and the stack.

The Stack Memory

The term *Stack* indicates a portion of memory available to a program, which is dynamic, but is allocated and deallocated in a strict sequence. Stack allocation is LIFO (Last In, First Out). This means that the last memory object you've allocated will be the first to be deleted. Stack memory is typically used by routines (procedure, function, and method calls) for parameters and local variables.

When you call a routine, its parameters and return type are placed on the stack (unless you optimize the call, as Delphi does by default). Also the variables you declare within a routine (using a var block before the begin statement) are stored on the stack, so that when the routine terminates they'll be automatically removed (before getting back to the calling routine, in LIFO order).

Pascal uses the stack for routine parameters and return values (unless you set the default register calling convention), for local routine variables, for Windows API function calls, and so on.

Applications can reserve a large amount of memory for the stack. In Delphi you set this in the linker page of the project options, however, the default is generally sufficient. If you ever receive a stack full error message this is probably because you have a function recursively calling itself forever, not because the stack space is too limited.

The Heap Memory

The term *Heap* indicates a portion of memory available to a program, also called the dynamic memory area. The heap is the area in which the allocation and deallocation of memory happens in random order. This means that if you allocate three blocks of memory in sequence, they can be destroyed later on in any order. The heap manager (or memory manager) takes care of all the details for you, so you simply ask for new memory with GetMem or by calling a constructor to create an object, and the runtime will return you a new memory block (optionally reusing memory blocks already discarded).

Pascal uses the heap for allocating the memory of each and every object, the text of the strings, the content of dynamic arrays, and for specific custom requests of dynamic memory. Windows, for example, allows an application to have up to 2 GigaBytes of address space, most of which can be used by the heap.

Dynamic Arrays

Traditionally, the Pascal language has always had fixed-size arrays. When you declare a data type using the array construct, you have to specify the number of elements of the array. As expert programmers probably know, there were a few techniques you could use to implement dynamic arrays, typically using pointers and manually allocating and freeing the required memory.

Delphi 4 introduced a very simple implementation of dynamic arrays, modeling them after the dynamic long string type I've just covered. As long strings, dynamic arrays are dynamically allocated and reference counted, but they do not offer a copy-on-write technique. You can deallocate an array by setting its variable to nil or its length to zero.

You can simply declare an array without specifying the number of elements and then allocate it with a given size using the SetLength procedure. The same procedure can also be used to resize an array without losing its content. There are also other string-inspired procedures, such as the Copy function, that you can use on arrays. Here is a small code excerpt, underscoring the fact that you must both declare and allocate memory for the array before you can start using it:

```
var
  Array1: array of Integer;
begin
  Array1 [1] := 100; // error
  SetLength (Array1, 100);
  Array1 [99] := 100; // OK
end;
```

As you indicate only the number of elements of the array, the index invariably starts from 0. Generic arrays in Pascal allow a non-zero low bound and non-integer indexes, two features that dynamic arrays don't support. To learn about the status of a dynamic array, you can use the Length, High, and Low functions, as with any other array. For dynamic arrays, however, Low always returns 0, and High always returns the length minus one. This implies that for an empty array High returns -1 (which, when you think about it, is a strange value, as it is lower than that returned by Low).

After this short introduction I can show you a simple example, called DynArr. It is indeed simple because there is nothing very complex about dynamic arrays. I'll also use it to show a few possible errors programmers might make. The program declares two global arrays and initializes the first as it starts:

```
var
  Array1, Array2: array of Integer;

begin
  // allocate
  SetLength (Array1, 100);
```

This sets all the values to zero. The initialization code makes it possible to start reading and writing values of the array right away, without any fear of memory errors. (Assuming, of course, that you don't try to access items beyond the upper bound of the array.) For an even better initialization, the program has further code that writes into each cell of the array:

```
var
  I: Integer;
begin
  for I := Low (Array1) to High (Array1) do
    Array1 [I] := I;
```

By calling SetLength again, you can modify the size of the array without losing its contents. You can test this reading a value:

```
  // grow keeping existing values
  SetLength (Array1, 200);

  // extract
  writeln(IntToStr (Array1 [99]));
```

The only slightly complex code is in the final part of the program, which copies one array to the other one with the := operator, effectively creating an alias (a new variable referring to the same array in memory). At this point, however, if you modify one of the arrays, the other is affected as well, as they both refer to the same memory area:

```
  // alias
  Array2 := Array1;
```

```
// change one (both change)
Array2 [99] := 1000;

// show the other
writeln (IntToStr (Array1 [99]));
```

At this point the sample program does two more operations. The first is an equality test on the arrays. This doesn't tests the actual elements of the structures, but rather the memory areas the arrays refer to, checking whether the variables are two aliases of the same array in memory:

```
if Array1 = Array2 then
  Beep;

// truncate first array
Array1 := Copy (Array2, 0, 10);
```

The second is a call to the Copy function, which not only copies data from one array to the other, but also replaces the first array with a new one created by the function. The effect is that the Array1 variable now refers to an array of 11 elements, so that asking for value 99 again will produce a memory error and raise an exception (unless you have range-checking turned off, in which case the error remains but the exception is not displayed).

Summary

This chapter introduced the role of different memory areas and covers dynamic arrays, an important element for memory management. The next Chapter will focus on bare-bone Windows applications, the following covers an extension to the core Pascal language, the Variant data type.

Chapter 9: Windows Programming

Delphi provides complete encapsulation of the low-level Windows API using Object Pascal and the Visual Component Library (VCL)[47]. It is rarely necessary to build Windows applications using plain Pascal and calling Windows API functions directly. Nevertheless, programmers who want to use some special techniques not supported by the VCL or who don't want to use a visual environment still have that option.

As this book focuses on Pascal, I'll show you how you could build a Pascal Windows application, an excuse for learning some of the core features of the operating system, something useful even when using a high-level framework. You can build Pascal Linux and Mac OS X applications in a similar fashion by accessing a different API such as GTK 2 under Linux and Carbon for Mac OSX. The principles are the same but I'm going to concentrate on Windows in this chapter.

---

47 FreePascal does something similar with Lazarus Component Library (LCL), which is on many counts a sort of a clone of the VCL.

Marco Cantù, Essential Pascal

Similarly, the principal of accessing the Windows API from FreePascal or GNU Pascal is the same as accessing it from Delphi, a few of the details may vary. You can check them out in the FreePascal and GNU Pascal documentation. So, I'm actually going to concentrate on Windows and Delphi in this chapter.

Windows Handles

Among the data types introduced by Windows in Delphi, handles represent the most important group. The name of this data type is THandle, and the type is defined in the Windows unit as:

```
type
   THandle = LongWord;
```

Handle data types are implemented as numbers, but they are not used as such. In Windows, a handle is a reference to an internal data structure of the system. For example, when you work with a window (or a form in Delphi terms), the system gives you a handle to the window. The system informs you that the window you are working with is window number 142, for example. From that point on, your application can ask the system to operate on window number 142—moving it, resizing it, reducing it to an icon, and so on. Many Windows API functions, in fact, have a handle as the first parameter. This doesn't apply only to functions operating on windows; other Windows API functions have as their first parameter a GDI handle, a menu handle, an instance handle, a bitmap handle, or one of the many other handle types.

In other words, a handle is an internal code (a sort of ID) you can use to refer to a specific element handled by the system, including a window, a bitmap, an icon, a memory block, a cursor, a font, a menu, and so on. In Delphi, you seldom need to use handles directly, since they are hidden inside forms, bitmaps, and other Delphi objects. They become useful when you want to call a Windows API function that is not directly supported by Delphi.

External Declarations

Another important element for Windows programming is represented by external declarations. Originally used to link the Pascal code to external functions that were written in assembly language, external declarations are used in Windows programming to call a function from a DLL (a dynamic link library). In Delphi, there are a number of such declarations in the Windows unit:

```
// forward declaration
function GetUserName(lpBuffer: PChar;
  var nSize: DWORD): BOOL; stdcall;

// external declaration (instead of actual code)
function GetUserName; external advapi32
  name 'GetUserNameA';
```

You seldom need to write declarations like the one just illustrated, since they are already listed in the Windows unit and many other Delphi system units. The only reason you might need to write this external declaration code is to call functions from a custom DLL, or to call undocumented Windows functions.

This declaration means that the code of the function GetUserName is stored in the advapi32 dynamic library (advapi32 is a constant associated with the full name of the DLL, *'advapi32.dll'*) with the name GetUserNameA, as this function has both an ASCII and a WideString version. Inside an external declaration, in fact, we can specify that our function refers to a function of a DLL that originally had a different name[48].

---

48 In the 16-bit version of Delphi, the external declaration used the name of the library without the extension, and was followed by the name directive (as in the code above) or by an alternative index directive, followed by the ordinal number of the function inside the DLL. The change reflects a system change in the way libraries were accessed: Although Win32 allows access to DLL functions by number, Microsoft has stated this won't be supported in the future. Notice also that the Windows unit replaced the WinProcs and WinTypes units of the 16-bit version of Delphi.

Marco Cantù, Essential Pascal

A Windows Callback Function

We've seen in Chapter 6 that Pascal supports procedural types. A common use of procedural types is to provide callback functions to a Windows API function.

First of all, what is a callback function? The idea is that some API functions perform a given action over a number of internal elements of the system, such as all of the windows of a certain kind. Such a function, also called an enumeration function, requires the action to be performed on each of the elements as a parameter, which is passed as a function or procedure compatible with a given procedural type. Windows uses callback functions in other circumstances, but we'll limit our study to this simple case.

Let's consider the EnumWindows API function, which has the following prototype (in the Pascal language definition):

```
function EnumWindows (
  lpEnumFunc: TFNWndEnumProc;
  lParam: LPARAM): BOOL; stdcall;
```

Consulting the help file, we find that the function passed as a parameter should be of the following type (again in the Pascal version):

```
type
  EnumWindowsProc = function (Hwnd: THandle;
    Param: Pointer): Boolean; stdcall;
```

The first parameter is the handle of each main window in turn, while the second is the value we've passed when calling the EnumWindows function. Actually in Pascal the TFNWndEnumProc type is not properly defined; it is simply a pointer. This means we need to provide a function with the proper parameters and then use it as a pointer, taking the address of the function instead of calling it. Unfortunately, this also means that the compiler will provide no help in case of an error in the type of one of the parameters.

Windows requires us programmers to follow the stdcall calling convention every time we call a Windows API function or pass a callback function to the system. Delphi, by default, uses a different and more efficient calling convention, indicated by the register keyword.

Here is the definition of a proper compatible function, which reads the title of the window into a string, then lists it on screen:

```
function GetTitle (Hwnd: THandle;
  Param: Pointer): Boolean; stdcall;
```

Marco Cantù, Essential Pascal

```
var
  Text: string;
begin
  SetLength (Text, 100);
  GetWindowText (Hwnd, PChar (Text), 100);
  Text := PChar (Text);
  // skip windows with empty titles
  if Text <> '' then
    writeln (IntToStr (Hwnd) + ': ' + Text);
  Result := True;
end;
```

The program calls the EnumWindows API function, passing the GetTitle function as its parameter:

```
var
  EWProc: TFNWndEnumProc;
begin
  EWProc := @GetTitle;
  EnumWindows (EWProc, 0);
end;
```

I could have called the function without storing the value in a temporary procedural type variable first, but I wanted to make clear what is going on in this example. The effect looks like the following (with dozen of lines I've omitted):

```
66762: ClamWin
66602: Interwise Push Client
66700: SkypeÖ - marco.cantu
66696: TrayIconManager
66676: HP ProtectToolsSystemTrayWindowInstance
66390: Windows Sidebar
66382: Apache Service Monitor
262732: TaskEng - Task Scheduler Engine Process
66022: HiddenFaxWindow
66018: BluetoothNotificationAreaIconWindowClass
131128: MMDEVAPI Device Window
196902: Battery Meter
131346: TSVNCacheWindow
133024: EnumTitles - CodeGear RAD Studio for Microsoft
  Windows - EnumTitles.dproj
132950: EssentialPascalv3.odt - OpenOffice.org Writer
262650: Wintech Italia Srl - Inbox (4) - Mozilla Firefox
133642: XanaNews 1.18.1.6
65780: Program Manager
```

This is a portion of the list of all the existing main windows running in my system. Most of them are hidden windows you usually never see (and there are also many with no caption that the program omits).

Marco Cantù, Essential Pascal

A Minimal Windows Program

To complete the coverage of Windows programming and the Pascal language, I want to show you a very simple but complete application built without using the VCL. The program simply takes the command-line parameter (stored by the system in the cmdLine global variable) and then extracts information from it with the ParamCount and ParamStr Pascal functions. The first of these functions returns the number of parameters; the second returns the parameter in a given position.

Although users seldom specify command-line parameters in a graphical user interface environment, the Windows command-line parameters are important to the system. For example, once you have defined an association between a file extension and an application, you can simply run a program by selecting an associated file. In practice, when you double-click on a file, Windows starts the associated program and passes the selected file as a command-line parameter.

Here is the complete source code of the project:

```pascal
program Strparam;

uses
  Windows;

begin
  // show the full string
  MessageBox (0, cmdLine,
    'StrParam Command Line', MB_OK);

  // show the first parameter
  if ParamCount > 0 then
    MessageBox (0, PChar (ParamStr (1)),
      '1st StrParam Parameter', MB_OK)
  else
    MessageBox (0, PChar ('No parameters'),
      '1st StrParam Parameter', MB_OK);
end.
```

The output code uses the MessageBox API function, simply to avoid including the entire VCL into the project. A pure Windows program as the one above, in fact, has the advantage of a very small memory footprint: The executable file of the program is about 18 KB.

To provide a command-line parameter to this program, you can use Delphi's Run > Parameters menu command. Another technique is to open the Windows Explorer, locate the directory that contains the executable file of the program, and drag the file you want to run onto the executable file. The Windows Explorer will start the program using the name of the dropped file as a command-line parameter.

Summary

In this chapter we've seen an introduction to low-level Windows programming, discussed handles and a very simple Windows program. For normal Windows programming tasks, you'll generally use the visual development support provided by Delphi, based on the VCL. But that is beyond the scope of this book, which is the Pascal language.

Next chapter covers variants, a very strange addition to the Pascal type system, originally introduced to provide full Windows OLE support[49].

---

49 OLE (and COM) are far too complex to be covered in this text. For some years they were core Windows technologies, and they are still heavily used, although Microsoft is phasing them out to adopt the .NET architecture.

Chapter 10: Variants

To provide full Windows OLE support, the 32-bit version of Delphi includes the variant data type[50]. Here I want to discuss this data type from a general perspective. The variant type, in fact, has a pervasive effect on the whole language, and the Delphi components library also uses them in ways not related to OLE programming.

Variants Have No Type

In general, you can use variants to store any data type and perform numerous operations and type conversions. Notice that this goes against the general approach of the Pascal language and is an implementation of a kind of dynamic typing such as employed in Smalltalk, Objective-C and may popular scripting languages including JavaScript, PHP, Python, and Ruby[51]. A

---

50 FreePascal mimics Delphi's variant type.

51 I demonstrated this "dynamic language extension" approach in a a talk I gave for the first time at the CodeRage II virtual conference in November 2007, covering "Domain Specific Languages in Delphi".

Marco Cantù, Essential Pascal

variant is type-checked and computed at run time. The compiler won't warn you of possible errors in the code, which can be caught only with extensive testing. On the whole, you can consider the code portions that use variants to be interpreted code, because, as with interpreted code, many operations cannot be resolved until run time. In particular this affects the speed of the code.

Now that I've warned you against the use of the `variant` type, it is time to look at what it can do. Basically, once you've declared a variant variable such as the following:

```
var
   V: Variant;
```

you can assign to it values of several different types:

```
V := 10;
V := 'Hello, world';
V := 45.55;
```

Once you have the variant value, you can copy it to any compatible-or incompatible-data type. If you assign a value to an incompatible data type, Delphi performs a conversion, if it can. Otherwise it issues a run-time error. In fact, a variant stores type information along with the data, allowing a number of run-time operations; these operations can be handy but are both slow and unsafe.

Consider the following example (called VariTest), which is an extension of the code above:

```
var
   V: Variant;
   s: string;
begin
   V := 10;
   s := v;
   writeln (s);
   V := 'Hello, world';
   s := v;
   writeln (s);
   V := 45.55;
   s := v;
   writeln (s);
```

Funny, isn't it? Besides assigning a variant holding a string to the s variable, you can assign to it a variant holding an integer or a floating-point number. Even *worse*, you can use the variants to compute values, as you can see in the following code:

```
var
  V: Variant;
  N: Integer;
  s: string;
begin
  V := s;
  N := Integer(V) * 2;
  V := N;
  s := V;
```

Writing this kind of code is risky, to say the least. If the string contains a number, everything works. If not, an exception is raised. Again, you can write similar code, but without a compelling reason to do so, you shouldn't use the Variant type; stick with the traditional Pascal data types and type-checking approach. In Delphi and in the VCL (Visual Component Library), variants are basically used for OLE support and for accessing database fields.

Variants in Depth

Delphi and FreePascal include a variant record type, TVarData, which has the same memory layout as the Variant type. You can use this to access the actual type of a variant. The TVarData structure includes the type of the Variant, indicated as VType, some reserved fields, and the actual value.

The possible values of the VType field correspond to the data types you can use in OLE automation, which are often called OLE types or variant types. Here is a complete alphabetical list of the available variant types:

varArray	varBoolean	varByRef
varCurrency	varDate	varDispatch
varDouble	varEmpty	varError
varInteger	varNull	varOleStr
varSingle	varSmallint	varString
varTypeMask	varUnknown	varVariant

You can find descriptions of these types in the *Values in variants* topic in the Delphi Help system. There are also many functions for operating on variants that you can use to make specific type conversions or to ask for information about the type of a variant (see, for example, the VarType function). Most of these type conversion and assignment functions are actually called automatically when you write expressions using variants. Other variant support routines (look for the topic *Variant support routines* in the Help file) actually operate on variant arrays.

Variants Are Slow!

Code that uses the Variant type is slow, not only when you convert data types, but also when you add two variant values holding integers. They are almost as slow as the interpreted code of Visual Basic! To compare the speed of an algorithm based on variants with that of the same code based on integers, you can look at the VSpeed example.

This program runs a loop, timing its speed and showing the status in a progress bar. Here is the first of the two very similar loops, based on integers and variants:

```
var
  time1, time2: TDateTime;
  n1, n2: Variant;
begin
  time1 := Now;
  n1 := 0;
  n2 := 0;

  while n1 < 5000000 do
  begin
    n2 := n2 + n1;
    Inc (n1);
  end;

  // we must use the result
  writeln (n2);
  time2 := Now;
  writeln ('Variants: ' + FormatDateTime (
    'ss.hhh', Time2-Time1) + ' seconds');
```

The timing code is worth looking at, because it's something you can easily adapt to any kind of performance test. As you can see, the program uses the Now function to get the current time and the `FormatDateTime` function to output the time difference, asking only for the seconds (*"ss"*) and milliseconds (*"hhh"*) in the format string. As an alternative, you can use the Windows API's `GetTickCount` function, which returns a very precise indication of the milliseconds elapsed since the operating system was started.

In this example the speed difference is actually so great that you'll notice it even without a precise timing:

```
Variants: 00.922 seconds
Integers: 00.005 seconds
```

The actual values depend on the computer you use to run this program, but the relative difference won't change much.

Summary

Variants are so different from traditional Pascal data types that I've decided to cover them in this short separate chapter. Although their primary role is in OLE programming, they can be handy to write *quick and dirty* programs without having even to think about data types. As we have seen, this has a severe performance penalty.

Now that we have covered most of the language features, let me discuss the overall structure of a program and the modularization offered by units.

Chapter 11: Program And Units

Pascal applications make extensive use of units, or program modules. Units, in fact, were the basis of the modularity in the language before classes were introduced. In a Delphi application, every form has a corresponding unit behind it. When you add a new form to a project (with the corresponding toolbar button or the File > New Form menu command), Delphi actually adds a new unit, which defines the class for the new form.

Units

Although every form is defined in a unit, the reverse is not true. Units do not need to define forms; they can simply define and make available a collection of routines. By selecting the File > New menu command and then the Unit icon in the New page of the Object Repository, you add a new blank unit to the current project. This blank unit contains the following code, delimiting the sections a unit is divided into:

```
unit Unit1;

interface

implementation

end.
```

The concept of a unit is simple. A unit has a unique name corresponding to its filename, an `interface` section declaring what is visible to other units, and an `implementation` section with the real code and other hidden declarations. Finally, the unit can have an optional `initialization` section with some startup code, to be executed when the program is loaded into memory; it can also have an optional `finalization` section, to be executed on program termination.

The general structure of a unit, with all its possible sections, is the following:

```
unit unitName;

interface

// other units we refer to in the interface section
uses
   A, B, C;

// exported type definitions
type
   newType = TypeDefinition;

// exported constants
const
   Zero = 0;

// global variables
var
   Total: Integer;

// list of exported functions and procedures
procedure MyProc;

implementation

// other units we refer to in the implementation
uses
   D, E;
```

```
// hidden global variable
var
  PartialTotal: Integer;

// all the exported functions must be coded
procedure MyProc;
begin
  // ... code of procedure MyProc
end;

initialization
  // optional initialization part

finalization
  // optional clean-up code

end.
```

The uses clause at the beginning of the interface section indicates which other units we need to access in the interface portion of the unit. This includes the units that define the data types we refer to in the definition of other data types, such as the components used within a form we are defining.

The second uses clause, at the beginning of the implementation section, indicates more units we need to access only in the implementation code. When you need to refer to other units from the code of the routines and methods, you should add elements in this second uses clause instead of the first one. All the units you refer to must be present in the project directory or in a directory of the search path (you can set the search path for a project in the Directories/Conditionals page of the project's Options dialog box).

C++ programmers should be aware that the uses statement does not correspond to an include directive. The effect of a uses statement is to import just the pre-compiled interface portion of the units listed. The implementation portion of the unit is considered only when that unit is compiled. The units you refer to can be both in source code format (PAS) or compiled format (DCU with Delphi), but the compilation must have taken place with the same version of the Pascal compiler.

The interface of a unit can declare a number of different elements, including procedures, functions, global variables, and data types. In Delphi applications, data types are probably used the most. Delphi automatically places a new class data type in a unit each time you create a form. However, containing form definitions is certainly not the only use for units in Delphi.

Marco Cantù, Essential Pascal

You can continue to have traditional units, with functions and procedures, and you can have units with classes that do not refer to forms or other visual elements.

Units and Scope

In Pascal, units are the key to encapsulation and visibility, and they are probably even more important than the private and public keywords of a class[52]. The scope of an identifier (such as a variable, procedure, function, or a data type) is the portion of the code in which the identifier is accessible. The basic rule is that an identifier is meaningful only within its scope—that is, only within the block in which it is declared. You cannot use an identifier outside its scope. Here are some examples.

- **Global hidden variables**: If you declare an identifier in the implementation portion of a unit, you cannot use it outside the unit, but you can use it in any block and procedure defined within the unit. The memory for this variable is allocated as soon as the program starts and exists until it terminates. You can use the initialization section of the unit to provide a specific initial value.

- **Local variables**: If you declare a variable within the block defining a routine or a method, you cannot use this variable outside that procedure. The scope of the identifier spans the whole procedure, including nested routines (unless an identifier with the same name in the nested routine hides the outer definition). The memory for this variable is allocated on the stack when the program executes the routine defining it. As soon as the routine terminates, the memory on the stack is automatically released.

- **Global variables**: If you declare an identifier in the interface portion of the unit, its scope extends to any other unit that uses the one declaring it. This variable uses memory and has the same lifetime as the first group; the only difference is in its visibility.

Any declarations in the interface portion of a unit are accessible from any part of the program that includes the unit in its uses clause. Variables of

---

52 In fact, even the effect of the private keyword for a class is not enforced within the scope of the unit containing the class.

form classes are declared in the same way, so that you can refer to a form (and its public fields, methods, properties, and components) from the code of any other form. Of course, it's poor programming practice to declare everything as global. Besides the obvious memory consumption problems, using global variables makes a program harder to maintain and update. In short, you should use the smallest possible number of global variables.

Units as Namespaces

The uses statement is the standard technique to access the scope of another unit. At that point you can access the definitions of the unit. But it might happen that two units you refer to declare the same identifier; that is, you might have two classes or two routines with the same name.

In this case you can simply use the unit name to prefix the name of the type or routine defined in the unit. For example, you can refer to the `ComputeTotal` procedure defined in the given `Totals` unit as `Totals.ComputeTotal`. This should not be required very often, as you are strongly advised against using the same name for two different things in a program.

However, if you look into the VCL library and the Windows files, you'll find that some Delphi functions have the same name as (but generally different parameters than) some Windows API functions available in Delphi itself. An example is the simple `Beep` procedure. If you create a new Delphi program, add a button, and write the following code:

```
procedure TForm1.Button1Click(Sender: TObject);
begin
  Beep;
end;
```

then as soon as you press the button you'll hear a short sound. Now, move to the uses statement of the unit and change the code from this:

```
uses
  Windows, Messages, SysUtils, Classes, ...
```

to this very similar version (simply moving the *SysUtils* unit before the *Windows* unit):

```
uses
  SysUtils, Windows, Messages, Classes, ...
```

Marco Cantù, Essential Pascal

If you now try to recompile this code, you'll get a compiler error: "Not enough actual parameters." The problem is that the Windows unit defines another Beep function with two parameters. Stated more generally, what happens in the definitions of the first unit you include in the uses statement might be hidden by corresponding definitions of later units. The safe solution is actually quite simple:

```
procedure TForm1.Button1Click(Sender: TObject);
begin
   SysUtils.Beep;
end;
```

This code will compile regardless of the order of the units in the uses statements. There are few other name clashes in Delphi, simply because Delphi code is generally hosted by methods of classes. Having two methods with the same name in two different classes doesn't create any problem.

Units and Programs

A Delphi application consists of two kinds of source code files: one or more units and one program file. The units can be considered secondary files, which are referred to by the main part of the application, the program. In theory, this is true. In practice, the program file is usually an automatically generated file with a limited role. It simply needs to start up the program, running the main form. The code of the program file, or Delphi project file (DPR), can be edited either manually or by using the Project Manager and some of the Project Options related to the application object and the forms.

The structure of the program file is usually much simpler than the structure of the units. Here is the source code of a sample program file:

```
program Project1;

uses
   Forms,
   Unit1 in 'Unit1.PAS' {Form1};

begin
   Application.Initialize;
   Application.CreateForm (TForm1, Form1);
   Application.Run;
end.
```

As you can see, there is simply a uses section and the main code of the application, enclosed by the begin and end keywords. The program's uses statement is particularly important, because it is used to manage the compilation and linking of the application.

Summary

Units were the Pascal (actually Turbo Pascal, as Wirth added the concept in the Modula-2 language[53]) technique for modular programming. Even if they were later followed by objects and classes, they still play a key role for encapsulation, for the definition of some sort of name space, and for the overall structure of Delphi programs. Also, units have influence on scope and global memory allocations.

---

53 For more information see http://www.modula2.org/modula-2.php and http://en.wikipedia.org/wiki/Modula-2

Chapter 12: Files In The Pascal Language

One of the unique aspects of Pascal compared to other programming languages is its built-in support for files. The language has a `file` keyword[54], which is a type specifier, like `array` or `record`. You use `file` to define a new type, and then you can use the new data type to declare new variables:

```
type
  IntFile = file of Integers;
var
  IntFile1: IntFile;
```

It is also possible to use the `file` keyword without indicating a data type, to specify an untyped file. Alternatively, you can use the `TextFile` type, defined in the System units to declare files of ASCII characters. Each kind of file has its own predefined routines, as we will see later in this chapter.

---

54 Notice that the `file of` language construct doesn't work in Delphi for .NET, as it is bound to the physical size of the date types it manages.

Routines for Working with Files

Once you have declared a file variable, you can assign it to an actual file in the file system using the `AssignFile` method. The next step is usually to call `Reset` to open the file for reading at the beginning, `Rewrite` to open (or create) it for writing, and `Append` to add new items to the end of the file without removing the older items. Once the input or output operations are done, you should call `CloseFile`.

As an example look at the following code (the IntegersToFile demo), which simply saves some numbers to a file:

```
type
  IntFile = file of Integer;

var
  IntFile1: IntFile;
  n: Integer;

begin
  AssignFile (IntFile1, 'test.my');
  Rewrite (IntFile1);
  n := 1;
  Write (IntFile1, n);
  n := 2;
  Write (IntFile1, n);
  CloseFile (IntFile1);
end;
```

The `CloseFile` operation should typically be done inside a `finally` block, to avoid leaving the file open in case the file handling code generates an exception. Actually file based operations generate exceptions or not depending on the `$I` compiler settings. In case the system doesn't raise exceptions, you can check the standard `IOResult` global variable to see if anything went wrong

```
  res := IOResult;
  if res = 0 then
    writeln ('File test.my created correctly')
  else
  begin
    write ('File test.my creation failed with error: ');
    writeln (res);
  end;
```

There are two rules to consider in the code snippet above. The first is that you don't need to call `IOResult` for every output operation. After a failure, following output calls will be ignored. The second is that the call to `IOResult` resets it value, which is why we need to call it once and keep the result value around to report it (by calling `IOResult` again for the reporting code will get a 0 result, meaning no error).

Delphi includes many other file management routines, some of which are in the list below:

Append	FileClose	Flush
AssignFile	FileCreate	GetDir
BlockRead	FileDateToDateTime	IOResult
BlockWrite	FileExists	MkDir
ChangeFileExt	FileGetAttr	Read
CloseFile	FileGetDate	Readln
DateTimeToFileDate	FileOpen	Rename
DeleteFile	FilePos	RenameFile
DiskFree	FileRead	Reset
DiskSize	FileSearch	Rewrite
Eof	FileSeek	RmDir
Eoln	FileSetAttr	Seek
Erase	FileSetDate	SeekEof
ExpandFileName	FileSize	SeekEoln
ExtractFileExt	FileWrite	SetTextBuf
ExtractFileName	FindClose	Truncate
ExtractFilePath	FindFirst	Write
FileAge	FindNext	Writeln

Not all of these routines are defined in standard Pascal, but many of them have been part of Turbo Pascal since the early days. You can find detailed information about these routines in Delphi's Help files. Here, I'll show you two simple examples based on text files, to demonstrate how some of these features can be used. The second example will include command line processing and is possibly the most complete example of the entire book.

Handling Text Files

One of the most commonly used file formats is that of text files. As I mentioned before, Pascal has some specific support for text files, most notably the TextFile data type defined by the System unit. In the StringsToFile example, I create a file (the filename must be passed as parameter) with some textual content:

```
var
  OutputFile: TextFile;
  I: Integer;
  Filename: string;
begin
  filename := ParamStr (1);
  if filename = '' then
  begin
    writeln ('Missing file name');
  end
  else
  begin
    // output the text to a file
    AssignFile (OutputFile, FileName);
    Rewrite (OutputFile);

    for I := 1 to 10 do
      writeln (OutputFile, 'item ' + IntToStr (I));

    CloseFile (OutputFile);
    writeln ('done');
  end;

  readln;
end.
```

Instead of being connected to a physical file, Pascal text files can be hooked directly to the printer, so that the output will be printed instead of being saved to a file. To accomplish this, simply use the AssignPrn procedure. For example, in the code above you could replace the line:

```
AssignFile (OutputFile, FileName);
```

with the line:

```
AssignPrn (OutputFile);
```

A Text File Converter

Up to now we've seen simple examples of creating new files. In our next example, we'll process an existing file, creating a new one with a modified version of the contents. The program, named Filter, can convert all the characters in a text file to uppercase, capitalize only the initial word of each sentence, or ignore the characters from the upper portion of the ASCII character set (those with a value of 128 or more).

The program takes two file names (for the input and output file) as parameters, plus one of these extra flags:

```
-U (uppercase)
-C (capitalize)
-R (remove symbols)
```

At the beginning the program parses the command line parameters, looking for the flags and for the input and output file names:

```
for I := 1 to ParamCount do
begin
  if ParamStr(i) [1] = '-' then
    Flag := ParamStr(i) [2]
  else
    if inputFile = '' then
      inputFile := ParamStr(i)
    else
      outputFile := ParamStr(i);
end;
```

As parameters are compulsory, before executing the actual operation required, the program has this test on the input parameters:

```
if (inputFile = '') or (outputFile = '') or
  not (Flag in ['U', 'R', 'C']) then
begin
  writeln ('Missing or wrong parameters');
  readln;
  Exit;
end;
```

The real code of the example is in the three conversion routines that are called depending on the parameters. The routines are in a secondary unit, FilterRoutines.pas. These calls take place inside a case statement, part of the DoConvert procedure:

```
case Flag of
  'U': ConvUpper;
```

Marco Cantù, Essential Pascal

```
    'C': ConvCapitalize;
    'R': ConvSymbols;
  end;
```

Once again, you can see the entire source code among the download sample programs of the book. The DoConvert procedure does most of the work related to handling the files;it opens the input file as a file of bytes (a file storing data as plain bytes) the first time, so that it can use the FileSize procedure, which is not available for text files. Then this file is closed and reopened as a text file.

The routine manages the input and output files, and then calls one of the three processing routines. Now, let's take a look at one of the conversion routines in detail. The simplest of the three conversion routines is ConvUpper, which converts every character in the text file to uppercase. Here is its code:

```
procedure ConvUpper;
var
  Ch: Char;
  Position: LongInt;
begin
  Position := 0;
  while not Eof (FileIn) do
  begin
    Read (FileIn, Ch);
    Ch := UpCase (Ch);
    Write (FileOut, Ch);
    Inc (Position);
  end;
end;
```

This method reads each character from the source file until the program reaches the end of the file (Eof). Each single character is converted and copied to the output file. As an alternative, it is possible to read and convert one line at a time (that is, a string at a time) using string handling routines. This will make the program significantly faster. The approach I've used here is reasonable only for an introductory example.

The conversion procedure for removing symbols is very simple:

```
while not Eof (FileIn) do
begin
  Read (FileIn, Ch);
  if Ch < Chr (127) then
    Write (FileOut, Choose);
  ...
```

The procedure used to capitalize the text, in contrast, is really a complex piece of code, which you can find in the example code. The conversion is based on a **case** statement with four branches:

- If the letter is uppercase, and it is the first letter after an ending punctuation mark (as indicated by the Period Boolean variable), it is left as is; otherwise, it is converted to lowercase. This conversion is not done by a standard procedure, simply because there isn't one for single characters. It's done with a low-level function I've written, called LowCase.

- If the letter is lowercase, it is converted to uppercase only if it was at the beginning of a new sentence.

- If the character is an ending punctuation mark (period, question mark, or exclamation mark), Period is set to True.

- If the character is anything else, it is simply copied to the destination file, and Period is set to False.

The following output shows an example of the transformation produced by this program:

```
// inputtext.txt
this is a red brown fox. the fox is
under a tree. GOOD for the fox.

// outputtext.txt
This is a red brown fox. The fox is
under a tree. Good for the fox.
```

This program is far from adequate for professional use, but it is a first step toward building a full-scale case conversion program. Its biggest drawbacks are that it frequently converts proper nouns to lowercase, and capitalizes any letter after a period (even if it's the first letter of a filename extension).

Summary

Although direct handling of files, using the traditional Pascal-language approach is certainly still an interesting technique, I strongly urge you to use streams (the TStream and derived classes) to handle any complex files in Object Pascal. Streams represent virtual files, which can be mapped to physical files, to a memory block, to a socket, or any other continuous series of bytes. You can find more on streams in the Delphi help file and in my Mastering Delphi book series.

Files management is a very large topic, and even sticking to the traditional Pascal techniques for managing files, one could write an entire book on this subject. But I'm out of space. This is, in fact, the last chapter of the book.

PostFace

At least for the moment, this chapter on files is the last of the book. Feel free to send me feedback as suggested in the introduction (newsgroup or email), sending me your comment and requests. If after this introduction on the Pascal language you want to delve into the object-oriented elements of Object Pascal in Delphi, you can refer to my printed book of the Mastering Delphi series (like Mastering Delphi 7 or Mastering Delphi 2005), published by Sybex, and my Delphi 2007 Handbook, available on Lulu.com.

Buying the printed version of this book or any of my other printed books (maybe directly on Lulu or through the Amazon links on my web site) is the best way to support my writing and push me to write more on Pascal, Delphi and also other topics in the future.

Helping me with updates, corrections and suggestions, is another very good way to contribute.

For more information on the latest edition of Mastering Delphi, the companion "Essential Delphi", and more advanced books of mine (and of other authors as well) you can refer to my web site:
`http://www.marcocantu.com.`

Happy Pascal coding!

Appendix: Examples

This is a list of the examples which are part of the Essential Pascal book and available for download in a single zip file (*EPasCodev3.zip*, about 30 KB) on:

`http://www.marcocantu.com/epascal`

Here is the list of examples by chapter[55]:

- Chapter 2: EssHello, EPExpressions
- Chapter 3: EPConstants, EPRange, TimeNow, Variables
- Chapter 4: Pointers
- Chapter 5: CaseTest, ForTest, IfTest, LoopsTest
- Chapter 6: OpenArr, OverDef
- Chapter 7: StrRef, FmtTest, StringAndPChar
- Chapter 8: NewMessageTest
- Chapter 9: EnumTitles, StrParam
- Chapter 10: VSpeed
- Chapter 12: Filter, IntegersToFile, StringsToFile

---

55 For more Pascal language demos and source code I suggest you look at the SWAG archive, currently located at: http://www.bsdg.org/SWAG/index.html

Index

www.ingramcontent.com/pod-product-compliance
Lightning Source LLC
Chambersburg PA
CBHW081129170526
45165CB00008B/2606